BEHOLD THE CROSS

MEDITATIONS FOR THE
JOURNEY OF FAITH

TONY KELLY, C.Ss.R.

Liguori

LIGUORI, MISSOURI

Published by Liguori Publications
Liguori, Missouri
http://www.liguori.org

Library of Congress Cataloging-in-Publication Data

Kelly, Tony.
    Behold the Cross : meditations for the journey of faith / Tony Kelly.
        p.   cm.
    ISBN 0-7648-0378-6
    1. Stations of the Cross. I. Title.
BX2040.K45   1999
232.96—dc21   98–45049

The Scripture quotations contained herein are from the *New Revised Standard Version of the Bible,* copyright 1989 by the Division of Christian Education of the National Council of Churches of Christ in the U.S.A. Used by permission. All rights reserved.

Originally published in 1998 as *Behold the Cross: Meditations for Lent and Easter* by HarperCollins*Religious,* a division of HarperCollins*Publishers* (Australia) Pty Limited Group, 17-19 Terracotta Drive, Blackburn, Victoria 3130, Australia.

Printed in the United States of America
04 03 02 01 00 7 6 5 4 3

Contents

Acknowledgments

I would like to thank especially the publishing and editorial staff of HarperCollins*Religious*, especially Cathy Jenkins who originally suggested the idea of this book to me. Then, at other stages, Susannah Burgess kept the various lines of communication open despite the elusiveness of her target on occasion; and without the vigorous and expert editing of Kirsty Elliot the book would not have advanced to its present stage, nor would I have attained a new level of humility. My thanks, then, to these and the many others, especially Fr Mark Coleridge, dear friend and colleague, whose inspiration and support make this kind of writing possible.

Foreword

Tony Kelly is no ordinary theologian. He is also a poet who under-
stands in deep and instinctive ways the language of metaphor. In
these reflections, he ponders the root metaphor of the Bible — the
metaphor of the journey.

For the Bible, our experience of God always involves a dis-
placement. In that sense, it is always a dislocation, with the
painful wrench which that suggests. But the dislocation is not
pointless. A journey has a goal, which is what makes it different
from wandering. For the Bible, therefore, our experience of God is
always a purposeful dislocation.

What Tony Kelly recognises here is that all the journeys of the
Bible converge in the great journey of the Way of the Cross. All
roads lead to Calvary — or at least all roads that are not dead ends.
Only the road to Calvary can become the road home to Paradise.

In *Behold the Cross* we find a convergence of three qualities
which have long marked the writings of Tony Kelly. The first of
these is erudition: we hear the voice of a genuinely learned man.
The second of them is devotion: we hear the voice of a man who
speaks from his experience of God. The third of them is
eloquence: we hear the voice of a man unusually alive to the power
and beauty of language.

In these reflections — as in so much of what we find in the
Fathers of the Church — theology, prayer and preaching inter-
mingle in a way which cautions against a too hasty drawing of the

lines between them. One implication of what Tony Kelly offers here is that the disappearance of one may mean the death of all three.

Suffusing all is a quality of *humanitas* — a grateful and good-humoured sense of what it is to be a human being, a love of what we are and a clear-sighted sense of our limitation. It is the quality we see so movingly in works like the paintings of Giotto; and it is this quality which marks the reflections offered here as Catholic in the very best and broadest sense.

Tonight Kelly sets over these reflections the motto of the Redemptorist congregations to which he belongs: *copiosa apud eum redeptio*. These are words which announce the overflowing redemption which is ours in the Crucified. The same quality of overflow is found in these reflections. They will prove an over-flowing source of wisdom and witness for all who seek to turn their wandering into journeying and to make their own way through the darkness of Calvary to the radiance of Easter. God speed to all who read them.

Mark Coleridge
November, 1997

Preface

Anyone who has a true devotion to the passion of the Lord must so contemplate Jesus on the cross with the eyes of the heart that Jesus' flesh is their own.

Let earth tremble at the torments of its redeemer, let the rocks of faithless hearts be split, and, now that the mighty obstacles have been shattered, let those leap forth who were weighed down by the tombs of mortality. May signs of resurrection now appear in the Holy City, that is, the Church of God, and hearts experience that which our bodies will undergo.[1]

These theological meditations on "The Way of the Cross" are humbly offered as one form of spiritual sustenance over the liturgical season of Lent and Easter. While I sincerely hope that all my fellow Christians, whatever their traditions, might gain some fruit from them, my starting point is the traditional Catholic devotion of "The Stations of the Cross". My initial concentration was to give new biblical and theological life to a time-honoured practice. You will notice that there are some fourteen meditations, somewhat freely related to the traditional "fourteen stations", but, in the deepest sense, covering the same ground. I have also borne in mind the new list of "stations" suggested by the Congregation of

---

[1] Pope St Leo the Great, Sermon 15 on the Passion, 3–4, as cited Thursday of the Fourth Week in Lent, The Divine Office II, Sydney, E.J. Dwyer, 1974, 190.

Rites in 1975. In that list some of the traditional ones were deleted as being without scriptural warrant (the falls of Jesus, Jesus meeting his Mother, Veronica wiping the face of Jesus); while others with a more secure biblical basis were added (The Last Supper, The Agony in the Garden, Jesus before the Sanhedrin, Jesus and the Good Thief, Jesus rises from the dead). The difficulty is to keep to fourteen! However, the main concern of any list is to mark the various turns and steps along the way of the cross which are significant for the journey of faith in which we are all involved. It is not an occasion to be too mathematical. Sometimes the heart runs ahead of the head in matters of faith, and no doubt is a surer path. But the head can make its plodding contribution, even here; and the result, dare I hope, will be new heart.

Naturally I have no ambition to replace the classic meditations of St Alfonso di Liguori, a Doctor of the Church, and the founder of the Redemptorist order to which I belong, and to which this book is dedicated. His expressions of inspired devotion still stir the Christian heart, and provide a model for the reflections, prayer and responses which ideally should figure in any communal prayer-service on the Passion of the Lord. The oft-repeated refrain, "Grant that I may love thee always, and then do with me what thou wilt" underlines the intense union with Christ the traditional exercise of the Stations of the Cross aimed to inspire. St Alfonso, "the most Neapolitan of saints, and the most saintly of Neapolitans" put his whole long life into bringing some warmth and devotion and pastoral balance into the Church of his time. The chill rigidities of Jansenism, to say nothing of the often destructive intellectualism of the French philosophes, had already begun to affect the warmth of Christian devotion manifested in a personal love for Jesus Christ. Alphonsus responded to the demands of his age, as we must to ours. We today have a more explicit sense of the world's ills compared to what was possible in the Kingdom of Naples in the eighteenth century. For us, the problem is not immediately how to serve God, but whether God exists at all. Biblical scholarship, compared to the straightforward devotional reading of past ages, has opened the scriptures to us in new ways. Yet the challenges remain, as does the beckoning presence of Christ the Way. The way of the cross still opens before us, as the way along which we find both the compassion of God and hope for ourselves and our world.

In this kind of reflection, one can hardly aim at completeness. I have usually taken some aspect of one or other of the Passion Narratives as the basis for a theological meditation in the light, or darkness, of our Christian experience today. The individual, as writer or reader in any age, gives only a tiny response to the Word that addresses us. Still, that effort to respond, however limited it might be, can enlarge the Christian imagination and evoke a dimension of feeling without which our hearts grow arid.

I recall an ancient liturgical collect that asks for "the gift of tears". It represents an affective side to our faith which has been somewhat neglected. But we neglect it at our peril. If faith and love do not engage our feelings, we have to wonder how real and how human our response to the reality of Christ's death and resurrection has been. And so we meditate, and pray, and try to bring to expression as best we can the truth of the Gospel, to arrive not only at the "right thinking" of orthodoxy, but also at the "right feeling" of authentic devotion.

My hope is that these meditations might convey some sense of how the Risen Christ continues to be present among us in our different journeys. After all, it is he who interprets for us "the things about himself in all the scriptures" (Lk 24:27). His presence makes us turn to one another, even in a time of great unfeeling, to ask, "Were not our hearts burning within us while he was talking to us on the road, while he was opening the scriptures to us?" (Lk 24:32). Footnotes have been kept to a merciful minimum. If anyone wishes to take their reflections further, let me mention, with gratitude, some of the sources I have found especially helpful in writing these reflections: Hans Urs von Balthasar, *Mysterium Paschale: The Mystery of Easter*, trans. and introduction by Aidan Nichols, O.P. (Edinburgh, T&T Clark, 1990); Pierre Benoit, *The Passion and Resurrection of Jesus Christ*, trans. Bennet Weatherhead (London, Darton, Longman and Todd, 1969); David Stanley, *Jesus in Gethsemane: The Early Church Reflects on the Sufferings of Jesus* (New York, Paulist Press, 1979); Raymond Brown, *The Death of the Messiah*, 2 Volumes (New York, Doubleday, 1993); Francis J. Moloney, *Belief in the Word: Reading John 1–4* (Minneapolis, Fortress Press, 1993); *Signs and Shadows: Reading John 5–12* (Minneapolis, Fortress Press, 1996); *Glory Not Dishonor: Reading John 13–20 (21)* (Minneapolis, Fortress Press, 1997); and James Alison, *Raising Abel: The Recovery of the Eschatological Imagination* (New York, Crossroad, 1996).

As you will notice from the patristic texts quoted at the beginning and end of this preface, I have occasionally quoted from "The Office of Readings" over Lent and Holy Week. These readings appear in *The Divine Office I–III* (Sydney, E. J. Dwyer, 1974). Such a device gives some indication of the wealth and depth of the tradition which is our common inheritance.

All biblical quotations used in this book have come from the New Revised Standard Version (NRSV).

Finally, I dedicate this little work to my Redemptorist confrères as they continue to live and suffer what they have preached in the spirit of our Congregational motto, *Copiosa apud eum redemptio* ("With him there is abundant redemption").

We shall share in the pasch ... for what is now being made known is ever new ... Let us imitate the passion by our sufferings, let us reverence the blood by our blood, let us be eager to climb the cross.

If you are Simon of Cyrene, take up the cross and follow. If you are crucified with him as a robber, have the honesty to acknowledge God. If he was numbered among the transgressors because of you and your sin, you must become just because of him. Adore him who hung on the cross through your fault; and while he is hanging there, draw some advantage even from your own wickedness; buy salvation by his death, enter paradise with Jesus and learn what is the extent of your deprivation. Consider the glories there: let the murmurer die outside with his blasphemy.

If you are Joseph of Arimathea, ask the executioner for the body: make your own the expiation of the world. If you are Nicodemus, the man who served God by night, prepare him for burial with perfumes. If you are one or other Mary, or Salome or Johanna, shed tears in the early morning. Be the first to see the stone removed, and perhaps the angels too, and even Jesus himself.[2]

---

[2] St Gregory Nazianzen, *Oration* 45, 23–24, reading for the Saturday of Week 5 of Lent, *The Divine Office* II, 246.

Preparation:
The way of Jesus

Before we attempt to follow Jesus along the "way of the cross" and try to enter into the dramatic story of his Passion in recognition of the love that has made us Christians today, it is good to pause for a moment to capture a sense of the whole gospel story, and the reason why it keeps on being Good News for us.

We must try to catch up with the fundamental movement of Jesus' mission, and retrace, however briefly, the steps he deliberately took which resulted in condemnation and death. It means coming to a sense of his mission, of the direction his life took, of the company he kept, of the truth he proclaimed — above all, of the God who was his life and breath in every moment and at every turn.

However we try to imagine the course of his life, there is no doubting that he was a man of startling freedom. His unreserved openness to the will of God made him free; free even with the most hallowed traditions of his people. His kind of obedience — though often idealised in Christian piety as little more than passivity — was, in fact, of a very disturbing kind. Indeed, it led both the religious and secular authorities to resent and fear his power. The force of his personality was both profoundly attractive and unsettling; the well-springs of his energy and imagination were fed by his conviction that he was acting in the name of God. The will of the One he invoked so intimately as "Father" and the whole passion of his life came together in offering the death-bound world such a fullness of life and healing, such a peace and a freedom, that we are still struggling to find words for it. It has been called "salvation" ...

In his fascinating presence, the accepted scale of values was reversed. Any religious law or tradition was made relative to the real love of God for struggling human beings: against those who implied, in effect, that God was indifferent to the hungry and the maimed, he would state with utter assurance, "The sabbath was made for humankind, and not humankind for the sabbath; so the Son of Man is lord even of the sabbath" (Mk 2:27-8). When the service of religion resulted in diverting support from the needy, his judgment on such a practice made him no friends amongst those had profited from such arrangements. His irony bit deep: "You have a fine way of rejecting the commandment of God in order to keep your tradition!" (Mk 7:9).

The compassion that marked his style of interpreting the traditions in the most liberating way meant for him a unique freedom of association. He met with and welcomed those who were deemed sinners and legally unclean. In this respect, he flouted the religious conventions of his day. As both guest and host, he shared the fellowship of table, such a highly charged symbol in Middle Eastern cultures, with all types and classes. In a world of so many segregations, he seems to have been remarkably accessible. His conviviality acknowledged no social boundaries.

Questions were asked about him. The guardians and devotees of the Jewish law, known to us as Pharisees, were a devout minority, dedicated to the maintenance of a distinctively Jewish way of life. In his unsettling fashion, Jesus had made it clear that he too was intent on the fulfilment of the law. But his methods were unorthodox, and even irreligious, to their way of reckoning. They interrogated his followers: "Why does he eat with tax collectors and sinners?" (Mk 2:16). He associated so freely and sympathetically with the legally unclean and the hopelessly sinful. He styled himself as their friend, a friend to those who were incapable of observing the law or even indifferent to it. He even numbered among his followers those who had betrayed it — the tax-gatherers and their minions.

In that world of factions and intrigues, he would eventually disappoint not only the Pharisees, but every group that tried to capture him for its purposes.

There were the Scribes, those learned in the law. They were shocked by the assurance of this unqualified Galilean. For he gave the impression of knowing what God wanted and how God was acting now, as present in the midst of his people. But these doctors of the law were convinced that God's intentions could only be disclosed through their scholarly searching of the scriptures. They were so preoccupied with how God had acted in the past, so intent on the glory of Israel as God's Chosen People, that they were failing to see how God was acting in the present to make Israel a sign for the salvation of the nations.

For their part, another group, the Zealots, were intent on freeing the Holy Land from the pagan occupying power. Fearlessly, Jesus too proclaimed that the reign of God was imminent. For him, it was only this reign that mattered; everything had to be staked on its coming. That message resonated well with the Zealots' intentions to mobilise the oppressed populace to armed resistance against the Romans. But Jesus was not notably anti-Roman. And when crowds thronged to him, he showed no interest in leading an uprising.

Though he accepted baptism from John, agreeing with him that a great turning point had occurred in human history, his way was in such contrast to the thundering asceticism of the Baptist. He saw the crisis of the times differently. God was not going to destroy his people for their infidelity. For him, there was no need to flee a doomed world to find God. The God that Jesus represented wanted to give a lost and broken people an impossible, unheard-of new chance, a new beginning within a realm of limitless mercy. In him, God had sought out the world; the Father had sent his Son, and those who welcomed him were destined to change the world as bearers of grace.

Jesus' style so differed from the Baptist's, and, apparently, his conviviality was so obvious, that he was contemptuously termed "a glutton and a drunkard", and earned a kind of nickname, "friend of tax collectors and sinners". For he was concerned to make God accessible — not to lock up the life-giving Mystery in a cupboard of impossible religion.

The Sadducees, on the other hand, were moneyed aristocrats, presiding over the Jerusalem establishment with a shrewd political pragmatism. They had learned to compromise with the imperial Roman power. As a rule, they supplied the high priest from their ranks, and were well positioned to administer the temple and its ritual, and so to exploit it to their financial and political advantage. The numerous pilgrimages to such a centre from all parts of the world, and the consequent demand for sacrificial animals, must have made this holy place a scene of roaring trade. Indeed, for the Sadducees all this prosperity was a sure sign of divine favour: in a harsh and exploited land, they were indeed much blessed. They had no need of any notion of an afterlife, they needed no resurrection to something else. But on this point, Jesus flatly contradicted them: "... you know neither the scriptures nor the power of God" (Mk 12:24). The God of Jesus "is God not of the dead, but of the living; you are quite wrong" (Mk 12:27). For him, to live with God was to live forever; the death-bound world did not imprison the living God in its limitations.

To this pragmatic, privileged religious group, Jesus was a troubling and intrusive element. His God, even though he recognised that his Father was "the God of Abraham, the God of Isaac, and the God of Jacob" (Mk 12:26), was so different from the way they imagined God to be. The contrast was driven home. Jesus championed the poor and talked about a kingdom in which these poor and powerless would be God's favourites. Such divine liberality struck hard at the Sadducees' sturdy convictions of rightful privilege. For them, the temple was enough: God dwelt there, and was usefully kept there ...

But Jesus, this layman from a disreputable province, was implying that God was immediately and easily approachable. He had been disconcertingly unimpressed by the importance of the temple, so central to the religion that served the Sadducees so well. He did not marvel at its magnificence and size. What caught his eye was the swindling and oppression of the poor pilgrims that occurred there. His anger blazed against the haggling of the marketplace as it invaded the house of God. He saw more true religion in the widow's mite than in all the rest of the extravagant panoply. For that reason, these guardians of the house of God saw Jesus as a dangerous and subversive presence, imperilling the status of the temple itself, to say nothing of their very profitable monopoly on its service. Besides, because of this fellow's influence with the outcasts and his growing popularity with the crowds, he was capable of disturbing the delicate balance of power so painfully negotiated with the Romans.

As for the Romans, they must have watched the comings and goings of this Nazarene and wondered what further problems lay in store for them in this maddeningly complicated, trouble-ridden part of their empire.

It came to this: Jesus was a man of contradictions. To the devout he appeared irreligious. To the learned, he was untutored. To the revolutionary, he was too idealistic. To the priests, he was a meddling layman. To the aristocratic establishment, he was a subversive intruder from out of town. To the Romans, he was someone to be watched ...

It seems that nobody could understand him except those whom no one cared about — those whom he called "the poor", "the least", "the little ones", "the lost sheep of the house of Israel". These groups are described at different times as sinners, prostitutes, lepers, beggars, as the diseased and the crippled, the hungry, the widowed and the orphaned — all those who had no place in a society that had used its religion to dehumanise itself.

In such disreputable company, he seems to have made God real in a way that religion could not. He did not so much explain God, let alone teach a new theology. He simply involved God in what he said and did. A kind of springtime of joyous, hopeful conviction seemed to radiate from him. Everything he said and did, the very way he stretched out his hands in healing to those who were brought to him, the way he blessed and forgave those who thought of themselves as being outside the reach of any mercy — all this was concentrated on one thing: to provoke faith and an unreserved surrender to the wonder of divine grace and mercy.

11

In his way of imagining the world, what finally mattered in human life was not your virtue, nor your guilt; not your social position, nor your achievements; certainly not your possessions. It was your faith that mattered — that fundamental openness of heart before God: "All things can be done for the one who believes" (Mk 9:23b). Let God and his overwhelming salvation into your life, then mountains will move, blind eyes will see and deaf ears hear, the maimed will dance, and demons will be driven out. Nothing would be impossible. Even the rich could get into heaven!

This most convivial of men used the setting of his meals with the poor and disreputable to speak of the future in terms of the joy of a great banquet to which all are invited (Lk 14:15). There, all will be made welcome; no one need feel excluded — unless they set themselves apart from the joy of the feast and refused to imitate the generosity of the host.

In all this he made God real as no one else had done. With easy assurance, he spoke and acted in the name of the One he invoked as "Abba, Father". He moved and worked in the power of a Holy Spirit through which he drove out evil spirits from the afflicted and possessed.

In what sense was God in him? How did God enter into his very identity as "Beloved Son of God"? These were questions kept for later ages when the doctrines of the Church would try to catch up with the truth of who and what he was — the Word made flesh, the only-begotten Son of the Father, living out his identity in the drama of human history. Still, everyone knew then that in one remarkable way he was more than the great prophets of Israel: the gospels never present him as a man waiting for the revelation of God to be given. He is never waiting for the Word of God to be spoken. The prophet's, "Thus says the Lord", became in him, "Amen, I say to you". In everything that he was, without hesitation, he plunged those who approached him immediately into the world of God's deathless love and incalculable mercy.

If he was to be believed, if the One he involved in what he did was the Real God, if his power to act came from the Holy Spirit, then, in some deep sense, he was freeing God to be God — freeing God to be really himself, truly at home with his people. For Jesus rejected that familiar tendency of assigning God a respectable place in an inhuman world. His mission was to lead human beings, no matter what their brokenness and guilt, into the universe of grace, that realm of real life which he called the kingdom of God, his Father.

In him, God was breaking out of the captivity of the constrictions of hallowed traditions, sacred institutions and exclusive groups into an immediate and wondrous contact with human beings in their struggling lives. The living, saving mystery of God could no longer be enclosed; love had broken out. The light shone and darkness could not overcome it.

In that light Jesus imagined the world differently. He delivered the fruit of his imagination through parables — deeply ironic invitations to enter the universe as God sees it. These sharp and provocative little stories and figures were precisely calculated to make people see their ordinary world upside down. Thus, it is a strange world disclosed to any God-fearing Jew to find that a Samaritan could be good; that a shepherd could leave ninety-nine sheep to look for one that was lost; that a patriarch could make himself ridiculous by feting the return of a worthless son; that a hard-nosed businessman could be so sentimental as to write off the debts of a shifty manager ...

In the world of Jesus there was room for a kind of divine folly. It was the world of impossible chances. Here, what society thought mattered did not matter at all. Here, the last was to be the first, the least to be numbered among the wisest, and the sinner was the beloved of God. If you had faith and let God really be God, then your world just had to change. In making room for such a God, you had to make room for everyone. If you came to accept that God was uncalculating in his goodness, then you had to be too: forgiving seventy times seven, loving your enemies, turning the other cheek, being generous and expecting nothing in return, while leaving all judgment to an ultimate mercy. It was all rather wonderfully foolish; but that is what Jesus implied that God was like — not really interested in your wealth and your status; not necessarily impressed with your virtue and sacrifices; not even put off by your sins!

The real God wanted only your faith. For if you had that, the God could act; and you could have everything. If you were capable of asking and seeking and knocking at the door, you would be all right. You would receive. You would find. The door would finally be opened. The mountains would move. Being anxious about yourself only blinded you to the joyous extent and superabundance of the kingdom being offered to you. Faith was the way into the truth that made you free.

It was all so new and intoxicating. The new wine bubbled in the old bottles. Loving God now meant loving everyone. Honouring the God who was "our Father" now meant caring for the least, the powerless, having hope for the hopeless. The poor, the manifestly God-forsaken, mattered as much as you did — and more than you, if you thought you were better than they were. The newness of the kingdom Jesus spoke of wondrously exploded all the old limits: all those self-centred, closed little worlds now had to yield to the limitless generosity of God's universe.

Of course, it was all too much. He had to go. He had to go if anyone was to survive in peace. So the various factions found common cause in plotting his death. In the end, a disciple betrayed him; and the Romans, after some hesitation, carried out the political solution to the problem he posed.

His execution was devastating to those who had been captivated by this fascinating man. The springtime of those months of pure energy and joy and love for everyone ended on that bleak day. It was all blown away, like the flowers of the field that he had loved. He had said in a final loving meal with those closest to him that his blood was about to be poured out for the cause that had occupied his every living moment. And so it happened.

Who was to blame? Who could sleep easy as that night came down? It is true that one of his disciples, Judas, had betrayed him to the parties plotting during these months to destroy him. They hand him over to the Jewish leaders. From the Sanhedrin he is taken to the Roman governor. Pilate passes him along to the local puppet king. Herod sends him back to Pilate. The Governor offers him to the mercy of the mob. Betrayed by one of his own, denied by the leader of those he had chosen to walk with him, left for lost by the rest of them, despised now by his own people, libelled by false witnesses, he is condemned in the courts of the secular and religious authorities alike. Then, after being tortured by the police and soldiers guarding him, he is executed in the hideous manner of crucifixion. He had spoken little in his defence, and in the end remained completely silent. What he had to say had all been said.

A radiant life-giving goodness was thus swallowed up in mortal darkness. In death, he was wrapped around with all the shrouds of that darkness: abandonment and rejection by his chosen followers; condemnation by every authority in his world; prolonged obscene humiliating torture; utter failure. All he had lived for was ending in defeat. At this point of intense isolation, he felt the most dreadful darkness of all: the One whom he had so lovingly and easily invoked as "his Father", the God of the welcoming love and limitless mercy, where was he now in this God-forsaken moment?

One of the most tender memories that lived on in the hearts of his disciples was of a half-groaning exchange between him and one of those crucified with him. It had to be a joke. One of the condemned murmured, "Jesus, remember me when you come into your kingdom" (Lk 23:42). A magical humour never deserted Jesus, that ability to tease both the small and great into not taking themselves too seriously. This time it was indeed strange: "Today you will be with me in Paradise" (v. 43). But, then that last cry ... and it was over.

In a number of hiding places, those who had once followed him with joy now passed hours of fear and dumb, unspeakable grief. Through it all they were left with one tiny consolation. It never could have worked, really. The real world was too old and wise to be duped by such folly. Life was too bleak and hard for such a beautiful dream. Of course, Jesus had to fail. But life had to go on. So they planned their escape, and began to talk about Galilee and the boats and nets they had left there.

What happened after that we will never clearly know. Even if at the deepest level of the heart we feel we do know, we can never expect to find the words to describe the utterly novel and unexpected event that disclosed him as living, now transformed among them, present to these who had experienced his execution as the destruction of all their hopes. It was certainly Jesus, they all agreed — no one else. He lived! They were dead sure of that. He lived — even while bearing the marks of that terrible cross.

His return from the dark domain of the dead released an unfathomable joy. That, too, is clear. Yet, we must suspect, it was mixed with a special kind of fear, even dread. Because, if he were really alive, if death had been vanquished in him, if God were so real and so intimately and passionately involved with his followers, then here was the truth that made all the difference. And none of us whose lives he touches can ever rest in peace again.

I

Jesus washes
the disciples' feet

The explicit story of the Passion of the Lord rightly begins on Holy Thursday. On the evening of this day, the meal that Christian devotion has traditionally called "the Last Supper" is held. It leads later that night to the "Agony in the Garden" and to the arrest, imprisonment and cross-examination of Jesus. After this meal, in what will happen later this night and on the morrow — his final day — Jesus will speak little, and even do little. He will be borne along by the events that overtake him and send him to his death.

But at this final meal with those who have stayed with him to this point, in gesture and word he will express the whole mission of his life and his deepest consciousness of what has been going on and of what is about to take place. He will draw those with him into the deepest desires of his heart and share with them his way of imagining the world far otherwise than those who are about to imprison, condemn, torture and execute him.

In the months and years to come, the disciples, who were with him at table in these hours as the darkness of that night thickened about them, would treasure memories of this final meal. And in the light of the great change that would affect all who followed him, the earliest believers would remember his words, "Do this in memory of me".

He whose memory they celebrated had lived so differently. His every breath was a protest against the envy and violence which had given death its power to chill the human heart and to hide our world in its shadow. In our fear and despair and suspicion of God we human beings have all been complicit in the reign of death and dwelt in the shadow of death. But Jesus' life was different. "The God of the living", the Father from whom he came, whose reign he proclaimed, whom he had loved with all his heart and with all his soul, with all his mind and with all his strength, was the won-drously merciful space in which life would be revealed in its deepest meaning. God was the ever-present and final reality, the life-giver judging and overturning all the petty idols enclosing us in fear and isolation, and inviting us into something more which could never be fully expressed or possessed — unless by living "in memory of him ..."

To live in memory of him had its own special implications and demands. To imagine the world as he imagined it, to feel for the world as he felt for it, to change the world as he sought to change it, meant to know and serve God in a new way. It would demand an unreserved surrender to the God who inspired the imagination of Jesus, whose love filled his heart, whose saving will was at work in all his words and deeds.

The gospels speak of a kind of divine necessity regarding the cross that awaited him on the following day: "The Son of Man must undergo much suffering ... and be rejected ... and be killed" (Mk 8:31; Mt 16:21; Lk 17:25). We human beings defend to the death the hard little world we have made in our image. Anyone who was bent on changing our death-bound world would be made to suffer and to face the power of death in all its ferocity. Anyone so disturbing the peace would have to be prepared to pay the price; to be sacrificed, expelled, to be violently removed from the scene where other powers were jealously in control. So Jesus was not really the victim of a blind fate. His fate was all too predictable, given the violence of a history notoriously inhospitable to its prophets. Nor was he the victim of capricious divine will only satisfied with such a death. He was not disarming God by offering himself as a sacrifice.

On the contrary, the true God, acting through the life and death of his Son, was working to disarm us. Through Jesus' suffering on our behalf, God revealed the murderous violence infesting our societies, and offered another possibility. What Jesus would undergo was the outcome of his passionate commitment to our real peace and to the humanity that God means us to share. In this respect, the clouds gathered about him, not over him from an angry heaven, but around him from a God-resistant humanity. For his solidarity with the poor and the lost, those excluded from the human table, brought its own consequences.

The old world, content to use God for its purposes, had no room for his version of God intent on making the world an open heaven, in which those content to live with God could breathe the free air of God's own Spirit of truth and holiness.

In the liturgy of Holy Thursday, the Church recalls two symbolic actions performed by Jesus on this last night: he washed the disciples' feet; and he gave himself to them as their food and drink in the bread and wine of the eucharist.

Now before the festival of the Passover, Jesus knew that his hour
had come to depart from this world and go to the Father. Having
loved his own who were in the world, he loved them to the end.
(Jn 13:1)

In the original Passover, Jesus recalled, along with all his
fellow Jews, how God had delivered them from foreign captivity
and formed a new people of God. The movement of what happened in that original event then reached its moment of fulfilment. There would be a final liberation, an unsurpassable
manifestation of God's saving love.

The decisive hour had come; all his life had looked to it. The
months through which Jesus proclaimed the salvation God was
offering were now to reach their moment of truth. The world
was to be opened to a new horizon of life. He was going from this
world bounded by fear and death into that space of endless life
and communion where his Father dwelt.

By leaving this world and going to God, he was not escaping
to a divine realm indifferent to our human struggles. For his going
to the Father was Jesus' way of remaining always with those he
loved in a final life-giving way: "unto the end" — not only to the
end of his life, but to the fulfilment of his loving relationship to
them. By being totally turned to the Father, in that heart-to-heart
relationship that had his life marked (Jn 1:18), he was to be turned
toward his followers in the world in which they were at once left,
and felt no longer at home. When he had gone, the home of their
hearts had to be elsewhere: in the house of the Father where he
was going to prepare a place for them (Jn 14:2). He was to be the
way they now had to follow (Jn 14:6).

It was the hour when love had to prove itself in the presence

21

of the forces of evil: "The devil had already put it into the heart of Judas ... to betray him" (Jn 13:2). The outreach of love is here confronting the intimate presence of rejection and betrayal. But it is not frustrated.

In the course of that meal, when the heart of the Son was laid open to receive all that the Father had entrusted to him — "knowing that the Father had given all things into his hands" (Jn 13:3) — in the hour that was to disclose the truth of his identity and mission — "that he had come from God and was going to God" — he expressed all this in a bewildering gesture. He did not call his disciples to some further act of reverence; nor did he reproach them for their failures, their incomprehension and weakness. In an atmosphere loaded with the anticipation of some climactic revelation of God, the disciples watched in amazement. He got up from the table, took off his outer garment, draped a towel around him, and poured water into a dish. Then Jesus began to wash the disciples' feet and to dry them with the towel around him.

Peter protested. The Jesus whom this leader of the disciples had chosen to follow, to say nothing of the God he thought to serve, would surely be dishonoured if he, Peter, went along with this! But once more "the Rock" (Jn 1:42) had to be shaped to another reality. What counted was not Peter's view on how his master should act. Jesus called him to go beyond his set ideas on who God was and what God willed, into another world of truth: "Unless I wash you, you have no share with me" (Jn 13:8). To be washed by the Lord was to be cleansed of the age-old encrustations which worked so effectively in keeping the true God at a distance. To be washed was to share in an alternative sense of God, and in a deeper familiarity with Jesus himself. It meant, too, that Peter had to find himself anew, by awakening to a new sense of belonging to others and serving them. The way of the true God was the way of love; and the way of love makes those who follow it take the lowest place, the role of a servant, that others might be washed and nourished with the truth.

It was not only a matter of having one's feet washed by Jesus, as though everything was revealed when the disciple was humbled before the humble love of God. For this lowly, loving service of others had to continue. Jesus unfolded his gesture in the question, "Do you know what I have done to you?" (Jn 13:12). In answering his own question that he had expressed in word and deed, he made it clear that we cannot use our religion to keep either God or our neighbour at a safe distance. We must allow ourselves to be drawn into the movement of divine life embodied in Jesus, to act as he has acted: "So, if I, your Teacher and Lord, have washed your feet, you also ought to wash one another's feet" (Jn 13:14). We can no longer love God because we love no one. We cannot serve God without serving one another.

In this gesture, Jesus is not simply giving us good example, proposing an ideal or expressing a sublime idea, the better to inspire us to treat one another with sensitivity and respect. It is that; but it is more. We are not left looking at him as someone external to our lives, but are invited to follow him in what was central to his life and its deepest movement: "For I have set you [a supreme] example, that you also should do as I have done to you" (Jn 13:15). The "life to the full" (Jn 10:10) that Jesus offers has as its central feature and direction the humble service of others. By sharing in his self-giving we are to be made like him: "Just as I have loved you, you also should love one another" (Jn 13:34). As a consequence, Christians can witness to the world. By being so taken out of ourselves, we form a new community of selfless love.

23

Only when our witness is made effective in this way will our world, locked into its habitual forms of self-promotion and rivalry, be surprised by the grace of another possibility: "By this everyone will know that you are my disciples" (Jn 13:35).

A further pointer to the meaning of this scene, at once so precious and so unsettling in Christian memory, is the teaching of St Paul when he invites the Philippians to "look not to your own interests, but to the interests of others" (Phil 2:4). He goes on to summon them to imitate the self-giving character of Jesus: "Let the same mind be in you that was in Christ Jesus" (Phil 2:5). The truth of the divine identity of Jesus was manifest in his unreserved service of others: "... though he was in the form of God ... he emptied himself, taking the form of a slave ... " (Phil 2:6–8). To believe in Christ is to "Let the same mind" be in us, both in the community of the Church and in all our social interactions with our world.

The other-directed love of Christ is the basic momentum of all truly personal life, both as it is realised in God, and in humanity made in God's image. In Christian understanding, to be a person is to be for others. Most profoundly, by performing this gesture of washing his disciples' feet, Jesus is drawing us into the "love-life" of the Trinity itself: "Beloved, let us love one another, because love is from God; everyone who loves is born of God and knows God. Whoever does not love does not know God, for God is love" (1 Jn 4:7–8).

The full meaning of Jesus' washing his disciples' feet will be disclosed on the cross. It is celebrated in the Church in the sacrament of baptism. In this water the Lord washes us clean and unites us to himself in his life of love. In the Church's liturgy, the mystery of love comes to its most intense expression in the eucharist. Through this sacrament, faith celebrates the gift Jesus made us of his body and blood in order to sustain a community of new and endless life.

II

The eucharist and
the Last Supper

In Luke's gospel, Jesus' last meal with his disciples occurs in the context of his many meals with different types of people. To a striking degree, he was a most convivial man. For example, he was an honoured guest at a great banquet put on by Levi, the tax collector, who had left everything to follow him (Lk 5:27–32). Devout Pharisees were critical of the way Jesus mixed with such company. But he reminded them that it was the sick who needed the doctor (Lk 5:31).

When Jesus was eating with Simon (one of these Pharisees) a woman of ill repute sought him out. To the astonishment of all, she bathed his feet with her tears, dried them with her hair, and began anointing them with precious ointment (Lk 7:36–50). When

Simon was understandably shocked at such extravagant intimacy, Jesus contrasted the cool reception his host had given him with the love that the poor woman was showing. He then proceeded to declare her sins forgiven, praised her faith and sent her away in peace.

When Jesus had welcomed the big crowd that had followed him out into the countryside, and the twelve were beginning to wonder how they could be fed, he insisted that the apostles share their own scant provisions. And so he blessed and broke the five loaves and two fish, and fed the whole hungry gathering (Lk 9:12–17).

In the course of his travels, after Martha had welcomed him into her home, she complained that her sister Mary was too absorbed with listening to him, and was not helping with the work. He reminded his generous hostess that eating with him was a symbol of something far greater than merely sharing in an array of good dishes (Lk 10:38–42).

When another of the Pharisees, having invited him home, expressed surprise that Jesus did not perform the ritual washing before the meal, he warned that purity of heart was the issue, not external display (Lk 11:37–41).

Dining with another eminent religious leader on a sabbath day, he gave a lesson on what that holy day should mean. It was to be a time for healing, not for ignoring the sick (Lk 14:1–6); a time for humble solidarity with the lowly (Lk 14:7–11), not for lording it over them (Lk 14:12–14); a time for open-hearted generosity to all, not for the calculation of social advantage; a time of openness to the gifts of God, not for distraction by lesser concerns (Lk 14:15–24).

Then, at his entry into the house of Zacchaeus, an exploitative tax gatherer, Jesus brought salvation with him. This hard man became a benefactor to the poor and a man of justice. One who had been lost had been sought out, and found (Lk 19:1–11). A story of many meals. Afterward, too, when the days of grief and fear had passed, his followers could only report his presence to them within the setting of meals. When the disciples on the road to Emmaus pressed the mysterious stranger to stay with them, he did stay, and ate with them, so that they could tell the others how "he had made himself known to them in the breaking of the bread" (Lk 24:13–35). Later, when he appeared to the apostles and a larger gathering of disciples, he asked for food to prove he was still the one who had eaten with them, even if now present as the Risen Lord (Lk 24:36–43).

The Last Supper, then, was, in a sense, a meal to end all meals, for it summed up all that he had taught and done before, and all he would become in the lives of his followers afterwards.

In its celebration of the eucharist, the Church is forever carrying out his command to eat and drink in memory of him, to draw from him its deepest life and love. The liturgical words are familiar. After giving praise to the Father as the source of all gifts and invoking the transforming power of the Holy Spirit, the eucharistic prayer goes on:

On the night he was betrayed,
he took bread and gave you thanks and praise.
He broke the bread, gave it to his disciples and said:
Take this, all of you, and eat it:
this is my body which will be given up for you.

When supper was ended, he took the cup.
Again he gave you thanks and praise,

gave the cup to his disciples and said:
Take this, all of you, and drink from it:
this is the cup of my blood,
the blood of the new and everlasting covenant.
It will be shed for you and for all men
so that sins may be forgiven.
Do this in memory of me.[1]

This is the "the mystery of faith" to be proclaimed in our lives: "Lord, by your cross and resurrection, you have set us free. You are the Saviour of the world" (Eucharistic Acclamation 4).

By remembering his self-gift under the symbols of bread and wine, we are summoned into the depths of Jesus' imagination and drawn into his passion to bring into existence a world transformed by God's saving love.

In his previous meals with the sinful and the outcast, Jesus had declared that it was the sick who needed the doctor. In the eucharist he gives himself to us sinners for our healing and forgiveness: "my body given up for you" ... "my blood shed for you, and for all, that sins may be forgiven" (Formula of consecration, Eucharistic Prayer III).

Long ago, that sinful woman of the city had washed and dried his feet with her hair, and anointed them with perfume. Through the eucharist, we are invited into an even deeper intimacy with him. He gives us himself to us as our food and drink, to nourish our experience of the forgiveness and peace that only God can give.

---

[1] "Eucharistic Prayer III", *Sunday Missal: A New Edition*, Collins Liturgical, London, 1994.

In an isolated spot, he had called on the disciples to share their meagre supplies with the crowd; and he multiplied their resources in a wonderful way. Now, the bread and wine of our lives is transformed and multiplied by him to feed our hunger, and to sustain the life of the whole Church in all generations. In the celebration of the eucharist, we too lay aside the busy preoccupations of Martha, and follow Mary, to receive from God the one necessary sustenance — Jesus himself, the source of the holy communion of all believers.

We too are drawn beyond the fixations with external ritual characteristic of the devout Pharisees, to receive from him that food and drink which alone can transform us from within — "so that sins may be forgiven" (Eucharistic Prayer).

The eucharist celebrates a new covenant as the culminating manifestation of the love and mercy of God. It leaves no room for proud ranking of ourselves above others, for we are united in receiving the sheer gift of God, love pouring itself out so that we may all be caught up in its outpouring — loving others as we have been loved.

In the eucharist, like Zacchaeus, we are sought and found; and salvation comes to us in the love of Christ, the gift that brings all other gifts with it.

In "the breaking of the bread", Jesus makes himself known to us at this later time. Nourished by this meal, we are drawn into his imagination; and in doing what he commands us to do, it is we who form the world into a new hope and a new sense of God. In all these aspects, he is still with us as the man of many meals, because, in that final gesture of love, he made himself food and drink for us in our journey of faith.

On that night, however, when the darkness was closing in,

there would seem little hope of salvation. While he eats with his disciples, foreboding and condemnation are hanging in the air: some great trial is impending. He will be abandoned to his fate. Where is God now? Only God can save him.

Yet, even on this night of betrayal and desertion on the part of his followers, he looks forward; beyond what is about to happen to him, out to what is to happen to them, and to all future generations of believers. His life even here is still a song of praise and thanksgiving, a dedication to the God who is acting in all the darkness that surrounds him, to the Father who is with the Son in a bond of unbreakable love: "He took bread and gave you thanks and praise", says the Eucharistic Prayer.

The bread; his body; our food: "take this and eat it, this is my body which will be given up for you." It is the language of ultimate love, to be the food of those he loves. He will be given up, eaten up, handed over, to torture, condemnation, mockery, death — food for those who too will suffer with him in the cause of God. His is a gift that will never be exhausted. For love keeps on being love, ever impatient with the way things are, a gift coming to us in the most humble of all the elements of our daily nourishment, yet now transformed in a giving beyond any human expectation. It is the gift we most need, that only he can give, that only he is, given right into the depths of our hunger and weakness: "I am the bread of life. Whoever comes to me will never by hungry ... " (Jn 6:35). It is offered to us where we are most starved of love, when we are so isolated in our separate selves that no one love can reach or call us. To a world starving in its capacities to be one in love and justice, he gives us the body of another humanity: "For the bread of God is that which comes down from heaven and gives life to the world" (Jn 6:33).

The wine; his blood; our drink: "This is the cup of my blood." The cup of wine he held in his hands symbolises that blood which will drip from his lacerated back during the scourging and run down his face after the thorns have been pressed into his head, and flow to the ground as he hangs on the cross; the blood of all his suffering, blood shed that we might live: "... my blood is true drink" (Jn 6:55).

Again the ecstatic language of love: under the transforming power of the Spirit, from the eucharistic cup believers drink the blood of a love without limit, of a passion that spends itself for the salvation of the world, of a life poured out "for you and for all". It is the wine of God's excess, of the folly of divine mercy. The excess of love meets the excess of lovelessness, that sins may be forgiven.

This blood is not the blood of violence or divine vengeance. In this blood, an infinite love, refusing to be anything but itself, bleeds, wounded and ever vulnerable to a world that sheds the blood of the innocent. This blood is mixed with the blood of all martyrs for the truth. Yet Jesus is more than one more innocent victim. Because of him, the blood of martyrs will not be shed in vain. There is love at work, greater than any power that evil can exert to murder and destroy: "the blood of the new and everlasting covenant". The blood that will be shed here has the power to bind the heart of God to the fate of our suffering humanity: "Those who eat my flesh and drink my blood have eternal life, and I will raise them up on the last day; for my flesh is true food and my blood is true drink" (Jn 6:54–55).

III

The agony in
the garden

In the days of his flesh, Jesus offered up prayers and supplications, with loud cries and tears, to the one who was able to save him from death, and he was heard because of his reverent submission. Although he was a Son, he learned obedience through what he suffered; and having been made perfect, he became the source of eternal salvation for all who obey him ... (Heb 5:7–9)

At the Last Supper, Jesus expresses his awareness of the arrival of that great hour when the saving design of God would be finally revealed. He has washed the disciples' feet, and gives himself to them through the symbols of bread and wine. As this hour begins, the gospels, in their respective ways, invite all who follow Jesus, in their own experience of suffering, to accompany him into a period of intense trial. Later in that night after the meal, his disciples, now mute and exhausted, are to witness his experience of a dreadful loneliness and abandonment.

They had adjourned to a familiar garden. Possibly they had left the city by going down the still-recognisable Roman steps adjacent to the temple area — just north of the old church of St Peter in Gallicantu — as they found their way to a plot in which olive trees were cultivated and an olive press (Heb. *Gat-semani*) was in operation. These trees were cut down during the siege of Jerusalem some forty years later. A cave at the bottom of the hill, where an olive press may have been kept, has been venerated since the fourth century. It was remembered as a place where Jesus had prayed in a crisis of suffering, and where his disciples were drawn into a drama which they would understand only later.

> Now is my soul troubled. And what should I say — "Father, save me from this hour"? No, it is for this reason that I have come to this hour. (Jn 12:27)

> The hour is coming, indeed it has come, when you will be scattered, each one to his own home, and you will leave me alone. Yet I am not alone because the Father is with me. (Jn 16:32)

For Jesus now it is the time of isolation. His life with and for others, all the years he has shared with family, friends and followers, all his actions on behalf of the lost and broken, all the words he has spoken to proclaim the presence of another kingdom, are now coming to their moment of truth. He can rely on no human support, no sympathy of disciple or friend, nor can he appeal even to the hopes of any time before this final hour ... The haze of images and projections and hopes in which others had attempted to understand and address him now melts away before his present agonising reality. He is stripped of all identities and relationships, save who he is to God, and who God is to him. The Son stands now utterly at the mercy of the Father. He is crushed under the awful demand to be who he was sent to be, in a world now moving against him.

The gospels poignantly record his experience of isolation. He moves away from those with him, into a grief they cannot share. After praying he finds them asleep, incapable of watching through this hour with him. In the end they will all flee.

It is zero hour in the drama of the world's salvation. Disciples and friends would go off, to be scattered in the loneliness of their own fears, disillusioned that things could take such a desperate turn. On Jesus they had pinned their hopes for something different, something new, something not known before in the darkness of the old world he had challenged ...

"Yet I am not alone because the Father is with me" (Jn 16:32). His aloneness is the solitude of the Son. At the deepest point of his identity is a pure relationship to this Other, the One from whom he comes, to whom he is returning, for whom he acts — and suffers. How will the Father be always with him now, when no one else has remained? He is torn between the agonising distance of two extremes. There is the infinite love of the One who is always with him, his Father, turned toward the world in its suffering and need. And there is the stony resistance of this world barricaded against the love it is being offered. Both forces work on him now; one as the will he must follow; the other as the threat that closes in.

He had given himself so "that sins might be forgiven" — that the old ways of living in loveless competition would be replaced by a new life of love and service, by a new way of being human drawing its hope from the way God is so lovingly divine. But before sins could be forgiven, those sins, and all the power of evil that worked through them, had to be felt and faced. It is as though he must let such evil do its utmost to reduce him to its own level, to break him with its power.

Once he had taken Peter, James and John up a mountain to pray. As he prayed they had witnessed the glory of the mystery hidden in his life (Mk 9:2–8). They had seen him transfigured before them. The brothers, James and John, had later asked him for a privileged place of honour in the future time of glory, "one at your right hand, and one at your left" (Mk 10:35–40). When questioned by Jesus, they had been confident of their ability to "drink the cup" that he was to drink, and to "be baptized with the baptism" that he was to undergo (Mk 35:38). Peter, likewise, had been convinced of his own strength: "Even though all become deserters, I will not" (Mk 14:29).

Now, Jesus calls on his once enthusiastic disciples to witness something different. Now, there is no radiance of the divine presence; no voice from heaven; no privileged converse with Moses and Elijah. On the mountain of transfiguration, the disciples did not know what to say because God was so close. Now they remain silent because God seems so far away. In that moment of glory, they saw in a new light the Jesus they had known. Now, it is "only Jesus" (Mk 9:8) again, but seen here in a terrible darkness. On the mountain, the Father himself had acclaimed him as the Beloved Son, and commanded them to listen to him. Now they hear only Jesus speaking of his sorrow unto death, praying to his Father that the cup might pass; and instructing them to watch and pray ... On the mountain their eyes were blinded by the light of God's glory. In the garden their eyes are closed in exhaustion and dread.

Jesus prays, "Abba, Father, for you all things are possible; remove this cup from me; yet, not what I want, but what you want" (Mk 14:35). The terrible pressure of this hour leaves him with nothing but the impossible possibilities of God. The kingdom of the Father, his Father's will, the presence of the Father in every living moment, all this had meant the world to him. Now the springtime of wonder and energy is turning to another season. He himself had asked the question: "How then is it written about the Son of Man, that he is to go through many sufferings and be treated with contempt?" (Mk 9:12). Now it is time to wait for the answer ... In that darkening world, how could the God of impossible possibilities act?

Yet he does not ask for "twelve legions of angels" to defend him and vanquish his enemies (Mt 26:53). He will not add to the violence of a violent world; even the armies of heaven would promise no other kingdom. His prayer reaches beyond what is, to what only God could be. He must drink the whole cup of the mysterious will of God. Only God can answer his prayer; he must let his Father bring about this other kingdom in a way not of this world. Love acts; but it cannot act in any terms other than its own.

Luke speaks of the appearance of an angel from heaven to give Jesus strength (Lk 22:43). As a result, "In his anguish he prayed more earnestly, and his sweat became like great drops of blood falling down on the ground" (Lk 22:44). In this beautiful depiction of the Father's care we are led to understand that heaven does not intervene to pluck him out of his confrontation with evil and waft him beyond the reach of suffering. Still, love does get its message through, even into the intense anguish of that moment. Only by his suffering the whole thing through to the end will the saving will of God be revealed. The heavenly messenger comes not to save him, but to give him strength to go on to the end: "having been made perfect" he would become "the source of eternal salvation for all who obey him" (Heb 5:9).

Yet all he can do now is give himself over to the divine will ... and be at the mercy of the forces gathering against him.

What he is suffering now will be the suffering of the Church in every age. There would be a million other Gethsemanes in which the followers of Jesus would be left with nothing but God and what God could do, in the face of insuperable evils and failures — when the world would seem so strong and God would seem so remote and ineffectual, and even non-existent. The words of St Augustine capture how we are with Jesus in his agony — and how he will be with us in ours:

> ... when Christ was on earth he prayed in his human flesh. He prayed to the Father in the name of the body. While he prayed drops of blood streamed down from all over his body. We read in the gospel, "in great anguish he prayed the more earnestly; his sweat was great drops of blood falling to the ground." Surely this bleeding of all his body is the death agony of all the martyrs of his Church. [1]

His blood runs down into the ground as will the blood of the martyrs who will suffer in his name. What will spring up from the great earth into which it falls? What Spirit of new life is working there? What kind of incarnation is earthed there as the life-blood of the Son drips into this ground? What kind of creation are the impossible possibilities of the Father bringing about? He knew

---

[1] St Augustine, *Discourses on the Psalms*, Ps 140, 4–6, *The Divine Office II*, Sydney, E.J. Dwyer, 1974, The Office of Readings, Tuesday, Lent week 2, 128–129.

what had to be: "Unless a grain of wheat falls into the ground and dies, it remains just a single grain; but if it dies, it bears much fruit" (Jn 12:24).

In the different ways the earliest disciples recalled his "agony in the garden", there are preserved memories and traditions about the way he acted in that dreadful time. The clear purpose of such stories is, as the Nicene Creed puts it, "for us and our salvation" — how we should act in the fires of trial.

Jesus is alone, but he does call the disciples to watch with him. There would be a time when they would go where they could not go at this moment. The words of John anticipate the significance of this hour for all the Church:

> Jesus said, "Little children, I am with you only a little longer ... Where I am going you cannot come." ... Simon Peter said to him, "Lord, where are you going?" Jesus answered, "Where I am going, you cannot follow me now; but you will follow afterward".
> (Jn 13:33–36)

All the followers of Jesus would have to bear the weight of this hour. For the moment, they could sleep; and Jesus comes back three times to find them unconscious of the drama in which they are involved. Out of his experience of the test, he comes back to strengthen them.

On one occasion when he was praying, the disciples had asked him to teach them how to pray (Lk 11:1). Now he gives them a final lesson. The prayer he taught, so familiar to us as the "Our Father", takes on a fresh intensity of meaning: it is a cry from the depths of the suffering he has undergone for us and before us.

He invokes God as "Abba", "Father". He has taught us to call on God as "Our Father". The all-enfolding mystery of God is the infinite love that works in all our lives. The God he invokes, the Father to whom he is turned, is the God who has given for our salvation what is most intimately his own in the depths of our darkness. This is no distant God, no violent God, but the God who is with us in our sufferings as he is with Jesus in his — the God who is not bound by the lethal violence of our world. This God will answer his prayer and our prayers. His Father is the source of the joy that no one can take from us; of the peace the world cannot give; of the truth that will set us free; of life to the full; of the love that nothing in all creation can diminish or subvert.

When faith is confronted with its most terrifying mystery, this Father to whom Jesus surrenders himself will often seem to be doing nothing. For God refuses to act in any way save the way of love. The creativity of divine love is above all other powers, and yet works its designs through them. Other kinds of power are making their presence felt. An armed company is coming to apprehend Jesus. Yet God does not act — not in any way that can be reduced to the powers of this world. Jesus prays, the disciples wait. No miracles now. Peter will strike with his sword. But this is not how God acts. That will be revealed only through prayer, only in the waiting, only in the full unfolding of the hour of trial.

Jesus returns to our sleeping selves to teach us the real meaning of prayer. To pray is not to manipulate God, but to let God act, in us and in our world. We pray, "Father, may your will be done" — not our will, fearfully operating in the tiny compass of our concerns and plans. It is to pray, "Be God for us — for our true selves, not for our defensive egos wrapped in pretension, but as your sons and daughters given over to your will. Be the God of our true selves, the source and homecoming of all that we are and of all that we share".

Inspired by the prayer of Jesus, we pray, "Hallowed be your name" — even at the expense of our own good names, even if it means we must pass through this world looking foolish and weak because we refuse allegiance to its idols of our age. "May your kingdom come" — not ours, our little kingdoms of violence, greed and rivalry. Let them go, and your kingdom come. Let all we are and belong to and long for yield to your reign, the realm of true and lasting life in which we will be found together. "Give us this day our daily bread" — not the bread of endless consumption, but the true bread of life, the bread that Jesus himself has given us, uniting us in one body of love and unity.

"Forgive us our trespasses as we forgive those who trespass against us." Let us not live by making enemies and counting the score of our hurts and debts. Allow us to take on your forgiveness, having hope for all, offering love to all, because you have forgiven us, and because mercy is the very atmosphere of your kingdom. "Lead us not into temptation." Do not allow us to crack under pressure now, but use the pressure of our times to crack open our world to your great and lasting peace. "Deliver us from evil", even as we suffer it, so that this "suffering produces endurance, and endurance produces character, and character produces hope, and hope does not disappoint us, because God's love has been poured into our hearts ... " (Rom 5:3–5).

Do not let us crack under pressure when the flesh is weak. When the tiny, timid span of our humanness tends to enclose us in defeat and fear and faithlessness, we know all too well that the flesh is weak, as we feel our distance from God and from one another, and drift in the aimless chaos in which our times seem to turn. Let the spirit, our openness to you and to all in you, be willing, and quicken in the willingness to be one with your will;

and one with the heart of Christ who has suffered the agony of our being. He suffered for us and before us: "for we do not have a high priest who is unable to sympathize with our weaknesses, but we have one who in every respect has been tested as we are, though without sin" (Heb 4:15).

From such prayer, patience grows. It waits for the fullness of God's kingdom to come. With Jesus, we wait for the will that extends through all time and space to be done in the whole of creation: "Because you have kept my word of patient endurance, I will keep you from the hour of trial that is coming on the whole world to test the inhabitants of the earth" (Rev 3:10).

From Jesus' praying in his agony the whole community of faith learns to pray. But the story goes on. It is not yet over.

The temple guard and the Jewish elders come to arrest Jesus, and Judas betrays him to them with a kiss. Peter, having resorted to a pitiful act of violence, will repeatedly deny his master in the hours that follow. The disciples "deserted him and ran away" (Mt 26:56) — stripped now, like the young man who had followed him, of every earthly hope (Mk 14:51–2). They are left in the shame of having escaped not only from those who arrested him, but from any involvement with him. They leave him, in an aching mixture of puzzlement, frustration and fear. In this dark hour, it was time to save oneself, not to wait on being saved in the way he had promised. Everyone for himself. Washing one another's feet and sharing in the gift of his body and blood were no longer real options — now that his body was captured by other hands, now that other people were after his blood: "The Son of Man is betrayed into the hands of sinners" (Mk 14:41). The reign of darkness had begun (Lk 22:53). Evil must have its way if the way of love were to be revealed in its own glory.

IV

Jesus before the Sanhedrin

Through that night, having been taken from the garden to the house of the high priest, Jesus is kept under guard in the court-yard. At one point he is interrogated by Annas, a former high priest. This supremely patriarchal figure, the father of four high priests, and now the father-in-law of Caiaphas (the present incumbent of the high-priestly office), embodies the nobility of Israel, the splendour of the temple, the power of vast political influence, as he confronts this strangely unsettling Galilean. Something has to be done. His son-in-law, Caiaphas, is of the opinion that it would be better to get rid of this Jesus if there is to be any chance of peace in the future. A dangerous situation has been building up:

Many of the Jews ... believed in him. But some of them went to the Pharisees and told them what he had done. So the chief priests and the Pharisees called a meeting of the council, and said, "What are we to do? This man is performing many signs. If we let him go on like this, everyone will believe in him, and the Romans will come and destroy both our holy place and our nation." But one of them, Caiaphas, who was high priest that year, said to them, "You know nothing at all! You do not understand that it is better for you to have one man die for the people than to have the whole nation destroyed." He did not say this on his own, but being high priest that year, he prophesied that Jesus was about to die for the nation, and not for the nation only, but to gather into one the dispersed children of God. So from that day on they planned to put him to death. (Jn 11:45–53)

Mindful of his son-in-law's convictions, Annas interrogates the prisoner: Who are his followers? What is he really teaching? (Jn 18:19). Jesus' response looks beyond the dark confines of the courtyard, beyond the reach of the guards that hold him prisoner. He has not been confined before, and would not be now. He replies, "I have spoken openly to the world; I have always taught in synagogues and in the temple where all the Jews come together ... I have said nothing in secret" (Jn 18:20). His message has been open to all. The truth he's uttered in the name of God is no political conspiracy; it has been addressed to everyone.

But not all have heard. Since it is rather late in the day to be asking him what he has been speaking about, Jesus refers Annas to his disciples. Despite their weakness and cowardice, despite even the denials of Peter, they have heard, and they know who he is. The lowly followers of this disreputable fellow have listened to that truth, and Annas has not. The message is not lost. One of the guards slaps his face: this is not the way to speak to such an eminent religious authority.

After this brutal humiliation, Jesus challenges the assembly to produce evidence of his lying or blasphemy or conspiracy. He asks, "But if I have spoken rightly, why do you strike me?" (Jn 19:23). Why, indeed? That question will linger through the night as Annas retires and Jesus is left at the mercy of his guards, who pass the long hours of the night tormenting him with their version of Blind Man's Buff. As they spit in his face and strike him, they see this mock prophet now reduced to silence and powerlessness. He has fallen into the right hands. He will learn his lesson. There is no defence for him now.

At dawn, he is led, bound and bruised, to a more formal gathering of the council of Jewish leaders. The reports of the trial which then takes place condense many of the investigations to which he had been subjected and the frequent disputes surrounding him in the months before. Now the charges are laid. With no one to defend him, biased witnesses tell their stories. They report how he had set out to destroy the temple itself; they tell of his pretensions to be the Messiah himself; and, further, that he has put himself forward as the Son of God, as though acting with a special inside knowledge of God's will. Through the proceedings he remains silent. There is no more to be said.

But then he does speak. When abjured in the name of the living God to tell whether or not he is the Messiah, this bound and brutalised man gives a shocking reply:

> You have said so. But I tell you, from now on you will see the Son of Man / seated at the right hand of Power / and coming in the clouds of heaven. (Mt 26:64)

He implies that two worlds are clashing — theirs, and his. The world of his captors and accusers operates under the standard of a violent and vengeful God. It is brought face to face with the world of Jesus. His world lives under the power of another kingdom. It owes nothing to violence. It is peopled by all who would open themselves to live in a realm of mercy, receiving and giving it, in the name of the true God. His judges are locked in another, narrower, exclusive world compared to his. In their world they presume to know how God must act and whom he would favour.

But Jesus addresses them from another dimension: "But I tell you, from now on you will see the Son of Man seated at the right hand of Power ..." Here his words resonate with the thrilling declaration of David, "The LORD says to my lord, / 'sit at my right hand / until I make your enemies your footstool' " (Ps 110:1). Certainly strange words coming from their defenceless prisoner whose permanent removal they are about to decide. And Jesus says the Son of Man will be seen "coming on the clouds of heaven" — a strange irony, given the situation. The only clouds around that day are the clouds of condemnation and death hanging over him. But Jesus is referring to the well-known prophecy of Daniel. The visionary had watched in the visions of the night and seen a human figure who would be the key agent in bringing about the saving reign of God:

> I saw one like a human being
>   Coming with the clouds of heaven.
> And he came to the Ancient One
>   and was presented before him.
> To him was given dominion
>   and glory and kingship,
> that all peoples, nations, and languages
>   should serve him. (Dan 7:13–14a)

The clouds of heaven represented the boundless horizon of God's universal grace, just as the "Son of Man" would embody the destiny of all who would live beyond themselves in surrender to God. To Jesus' mind, the destiny of Israel was for the salvation of the nations, not to restrict God to its own purposes. God would not be locked up even in the holiest of places, even in the holiest of cities, even by Israel, the holiest of peoples. By pointing back to this prophetic vision, Jesus describes himself as the one in whom God is acting. The divine initiative is not frustrated by the might of worldly kingdoms which had been represented in Daniel's vision as "four great beasts, four kings [which would] arise out of the earth" (Dan 7:17). In contrast, "the holy ones of the Most High shall receive the kingdom and possess the kingdom forever ... " (Dan 7:18). A new realm of blessed humanity will come as God's surprising and all-inclusive gift, not by human machination or force. By appealing to this vision, Jesus is declaring himself the fulfilment of Israel's destiny. In him God is keeping his promise of salvation.

Since Jesus had spoken of his mission many times before in such terms there was plenty of ammunition to be found by those conspiring to shoot him down.

He had proclaimed a new order of luminous access to God. Speaking with the Samaritan woman, he had at once placed himself within the history of his own people, yet opened the way to something more:

> Woman, believe me, the hour is coming when you will worship the Father neither on this mountain nor in Jerusalem. You worship what you do not know; we worship what we know, for salvation is from the Jews. But the hour is coming, and is now here,

when the true worshipers will worship the Father in spirit and truth ... (Jn 4:21–23)

In him God was being revealed, no longer restricted to a particular holy place, but as the Father known and loved "in spirit and truth". This Spirit Jesus would breathe on his disciples, just as he would embody the very truth of God. God was not a divisive force. The Father would not sanction the violence of exclusion and privilege.

When speaking to Nathanael, whom he had hailed as "an Israelite in whom there is no deceit" (Jn 1:47), Jesus had promised, "Very truly, I tell you, you will see heaven opened and the angels of God ascending and descending upon the Son of Man" (Jn 1:51). His disciples would recall, too, how they had puzzled over his reply to the guardians of the temple after his dramatic intervention to cleanse the old temple of its unworthy business. He had spoken of himself as the focus of a new access to God. He was a kind of new temple in the making, "the temple of his body": "Destroy this temple, and in three days I will raise it up" (Jn 2:13–22). He would be a new temple in which the God of all, the God of unity and love, would be revealed and worshipped: "No one comes to the Father except through me" (Jn 14:6). In a later prophetic vision, an early disciple expressed in striking language the implications of Jesus' role as the Lamb of God in opening up for all peoples a new relationship to the living God:

I saw no temple in the city, for its temple is the Lord God the Almighty and the Lamb. And the city has no need of sun or moon to shine on it, for the glory of God is its light, and its lamp is the Lamb. The nations will walk by its light, and the kings of the earth will bring their glory into it. Its gates will never be shut by day — and there will be no night there. (Rev 21:22–25)

But that was to come. In the light of his teaching, the Jewish elders easily found evidence of a deeply subversive factor in the words and deeds of their prisoner. In their judgment, he had struck at the central symbol of their history. He was undermining their very identity as God's Chosen People. He was contesting their exclusive authority to administer the divine law. He was set against them, the cause of conflict.

Such a conflict was nothing new in the history of Israel. Jeremiah himself had barely escaped death for preaching that the temple offered no security for those who had forgotten the deeper demands of God's law (Jer 26:1–19). Not all the prophets had been so fortunate (Jer 26:20–4). Nonetheless a call to conversion had been written into the history of Israel through its greatest prophets. More than any other culture or society, Israel, Chosen People of God, was aware of God's subversive witnesses. The great prophets such as Elijah and Jeremiah had been uncomfortable presences in their time. Most of all, the mysterious figure of the Suffering Servant (Isa 53:1–12) cast a long shadow through the centuries onto this moment of judgment:

I gave my back to those who struck me, and my cheeks to those who pulled my beard; I did not hide my face from insult and spitting. (Isa 50:6)

He was despised and rejected by others; a man of suffering and acquainted with infirmity; and as one from whom others hide their faces he was despised, and we held him in no account. (Isa 53:3)

Jesus had already noted the wisdom of the old proverb, "A prophet is only despised in his own country and in his own house"

(Mt 13:57). The leaders of his country and the administrators of his Father's house were reverting to type. Once more "it would not be right for a prophet to die outside Jerusalem" (Lk 13:33). The Holy City would witness once again how the boundless reality of God and our defensive efforts to contain it would clash, and a man of God would die ... "Jerusalem, the city that kills the prophets ..." (Mt 23:37). Such an irony was now sharpened to a final incisive edge.

Jesus stood there before them at the end of a long line of those who sought to recall Israel to a more pure and whole-hearted adoration of God; and, as a consequence, to a larger sense of its calling in the history of the world. How much did his present judges see him as someone utterly alien to all that they stood for? How deeply were they convinced that his words had to be judged as blasphemous because he had pretended to be so intimately related to God (Jn 10:36)? How much did they wilfully repress, in the pressure of this moment, what their own history had taught them? To what extent was the political situation so electric that any other considerations were impossible, and that it was expedient for one man to die for the people (Jn 11:47–53)? How much had they convinced themselves that God could not act like this?

It might be that such questions can never be fully answered. All that is clear is that Jesus had addressed them on one level, and they had heard on another. What he had intended for their salvation they had heard as undermining their security. Where he had striven to communicate the luminous universality of God's intimate and merciful presence, they found such a message subversive of all they held precious. Where they were holding to the temple as a symbol of God's presence to their people, he had dealt with the reality.

The tension was too much. Detecting a blasphemy, the high priest rent his robes. No further witnesses were necessary. The Sanhedrin reached its verdict. Jesus deserved to die.

If the complicity of the Jewish authorities in his condemnation were the focus of all the gospel accounts of this scene, it must be remembered that such a theme is all part of a larger sorry story in which no one comes out well. One of his own, Judas, had already betrayed him; the disciples had fled; Peter, the Rock, had denied him three times during these proceedings. Those who may have been called to be true witnesses on his behalf let the false witnesses do their work. So, now, the Jewish leaders embark on the final solution to the problem he caused.

Yet, there is a consequence. When his own people attempt to judge him, they find themselves judged. In its way, the history of the world, in all the succession of cultures and epochs, is written in the judgments it has passed. The human story is one of dismay at the manner in which societies do away with those who most challenge them to a greater justice. Meting out death to the martyrs who have refused to be complicit in our lies is the all-too-predictable expression of our fear of life. The removal of the innocent is always linked to our refusal to be summoned into some other way, to some other hope, beyond the violence of self-promotion and rivalry.

It is to the abiding glory of Israel that it kept alive, despite all the trials in its history, a sense of the promises of the one, true God. On the other hand, its great prophets were merciless in their exposure of its failures. It does not require any great humanity or humility to read these stories of failure with fear and trembling for ourselves. How would any of us have reacted in the face of external threat, with the destruction and desecration of the holy places, in the experience of exile, and, finally, in the reality of foreign occupation? It is a familiar human temptation to seek security in the way things are. There is a kind of safe peace to be found by looking backwards and inward, while God is to be found elsewhere. The fundamental thrust of faith pushes us to look forward and out, into the whole of history and creation. God is always greater. For the Jewish leaders described in the gospel story, nothing new could happen. Nothing new should happen — unless it work to bolster their secure establishment in the way things were. When they had possessed God as their own, there was no room for surprises.

In this Jesus, bound and silent before them, a familiar trouble recurred, far more unsettlingly, more unmanageable than ever. They rehearsed the possibilities: the Messiah had come? But they were still a subject people. A new temple? But this magnificent edifice was the glory of their nation. A new time of salvation for the nations? But they were oppressed by a ruthless Roman occupation. A prophet, and more than a prophet, speaking of God with such intimacy and authority, and declaring the will of God without recourse to their age-old wisdom? But he had put the temple in the shade. He had interpreted the law so differently, and had associated so freely with the hopelessly lawless. Dare they let go of all they had for the promise of some final new gift that would leave them dazed into a new world of divine generosity and mercy? Better to hold on to the venerable forms of the old religion that placed God securely in the temple, and themselves in charge of it, and all sinners excluded from it.

Either way, someone was going to suffer. If God were really the God of all, if God were to be revealed as the source of such surprising and uncalculated grace reaching beyond the clear boundaries of race and religion, that would mean a great dispossession for them. They would be seen merely as caretakers of the temple before this new thing happened. They would be left with nothing but what would now belong to all. Better for him to go, than for them. Better to keep God in the temple, a defence against the Romans, and a judge of all pretenders like this Jesus. He had to go.

In condemning Jesus, the Jewish leaders failed to grasp the astonishing grace that was at work (Acts 3:17–18). They were refusing to let God live among them in this new, wonderful, disconcerting way. In this their sins are our own. Are we prepared to let God out of the shrines and temples of our securities, to make us belong to everyone? Do we dare let God lead us, from a religion of self-defence, to be involved with all the victims of history? Dare we think of God so humanly, so scandalously involved in our darkness and weakness? Any answer at this point can be the outcome only of the long journey of faith: "God has imprisoned all in disobedience that he may be merciful to all" (Rom 11:32).

As for the people of Israel, one of their number, changed from being a persecutor of the Gospel into the apostle of the nations, expressed a great hope:

> So I ask, have they stumbled so as to fall? By no means! But through their stumbling salvation has come to the Gentiles, so as to make Israel jealous. Now, if their stumbling means riches for the world, and if their defeat means riches for the Gentiles, how much will their full inclusion mean! (Rom 11:11–12)

V

Jesus before Pilate

When he was abused, he did not return abuse; when he suffered, he did not threaten; but he entrusted himself to the one who judges justly. He himself bore our sins in his body on the cross ... by his wounds you have been healed. (1 Pet 2:23–4)

In the morning of that Passover eve, Jesus is brought by the Jewish authorities to the Roman headquarters. They are determined now to do away with him once and for all. As the temple functionaries are herding all the animals needed for the Passover sacrifice, events are now moving toward another kind of sacrifice, of another kind of victim, in another kind of Passover. Anxious to avoid ritual contamination on that holiest of days, in order to be free to eat the Passover meal in good conscience, his captors are careful not to be under the same roof as the Roman governor. Later, they will invoke Roman law to demand the full horror of

Roman style of execution. They will even declare, in the end, that Caesar is their only king. But they will not now be sullied by too close an association with the power of pagan Rome. And so Pilate comes out to them, and the interrogation begins.

Two interrogations in fact: the first, as Pilate searches into the motives of this maddeningly complicated people in bringing such a charge against this strange man who seems now so unconcerned about his own defence: "What accusation do you bring against this man?" (Jn 18:29). And the second — as he confronts the alleged criminal and tries to find out what, in fact, this Jesus is up to: "Are you the King of the Jews?" (Jn 18:33b).

The practical Roman administrator must have wondered what was really going on. Things were seldom what they seemed in this part of the world, least of all now. Why was this Jesus the cause of such bitterness and outrage? Pilate picks up some reference to him being a king: what on earth could that mean?

In the lethal sequence of events leading to the cross, the disciples would later remember another depth of meaning, then inaccessible to Jesus' accusers and judge: "And I when I am lifted up from the earth, will draw all people to myself" (Jn 12:32). What he was going through was not the tragic fate of one more innocent victim swallowed up in the violence of the world. His death meant something else; an event that affected everyone. Above all, it would open to the weak and hopeless victims of the world a realm of unending life. There, God would be revealed, not as locked in the temple, nor as guardian deity of imperial Rome, but as the God of another life, of communion with God and with one another. A judgment was being passed on the violent reality of a world constructed on human power and pride. The murderous lovelessness of all cultures would be judged in the light of what life really meant.

Pilate is not interested in internecine Jewish wrangling about kings and messiahs. Let these Jews sort out their own problems. However, it becomes clear to him that they really are out for this fellow's blood, and that they want official permission to spill it. An impasse: Pilate leaves them and confronts Jesus alone, to ask: "Are you the King of the Jews?". This strikes him as rather improbable given that the Jewish authorities are hardly interested in the coronation of Jesus as their king!

At this point the interrogator finds himself interrogated: is this your own question or someone else's? Pilate irritably distances himself from both possibilities: "I am not a Jew, am I? Your own nation and the chief priests have handed you over to me." As though leaving all this religious nonsense aside, he gets to the point: "What have you done?" (Jn 18:35).

In reply Jesus does not speak about what he has done; he speaks about something else: "My kingdom is not from this world" (Jn 18:36). Neither who he is nor the way he has acted can be understood apart from that other realm. His kind of reign is unlike anything on earth, unlike the powers of this world now conspiring to do away with him. His kingdom has no need of violent defence. The truth will come on its own terms. Another life-force, another power, is at work. Though his kingdom is indeed being realised in the world of violence and rivalry, though it is here present in the condemned and captive king, it is not "from this world".

Pilate, attuned to the vocabulary of political authority, lights on the one word that interests him: "So you are a king?" (Jn 18:37). Though Jesus speaks to the Roman in words he can understand — "You say that I am a king" — he now opens to him a horizon in which this other kingdom can have meaning: "For this I was born, and for this I came into the world, to testify to the truth" (Jn 18:37). The truth is about God, about our relations with God and with one another, about the all-inclusive kingdom present in the power of crucified love. Opposed to this truth are all false gods, the violence of our false selves, the lies that darken the world in which we live and breathe.

But there is another power at work. "Everyone who belongs to the truth listens to my voice" (Jn 18:37). Our hearts rebel in the presence of evil and its power to dehumanise our world and set us against one another. We can experience even our religion turned into a commodity to separate and victimise others. Yet a frustration with this leads to a deeper search, a keener questioning: what is the truth? What is the truth that can set us free from the miserable, doomed untruth of our times? Who can give us redemption? Who can enable us to break out of the vicious circle of vengeance which reduces our lives to a catalogue of unforgiven things? Can there be an alternative version of human history? Is there another truth set in opposition to the tale of hopeless bitterness which makes God powerless against us and incapacitates us in our ability to love? Must the little flame of good be snuffed out by the oppressive weight of evil?

All who search their hearts and hear these questions speak within them are listening to his voice. It stirs within us with all the great questions which will not be put to rest. The first words of the Word in John's gospel are the question, "What are you looking for?" (Jn 1:38). Are we looking for a truth that will set us free, a truth that will establish the sovereignty of love over capacities for hate, the truth of the one true God in place of our familiar idols?

Those who belong to the truth, who are looking for it, will hear this voice — the voice of one who is from beyond this world but has lived with us within it. He alone speaks to our hearts. He alone can bring the salvation that comes as the greatest of gifts, the divine self-giving itself. The source of all life gives what is most intimate to itself that we might live, beyond all lies, in the truth: "For God so loved the world that he gave his only Son, so that everyone who believes him may not perish but may have eternal life" (Jn 3:16). To encounter Jesus means an ultimate choice: either to be nourished by the life-giving truth he embodies, or to be devoured by the falsehood of endless self-justification.

But now the reality of God's truth is at once offered — and missed. Pilate asks Jesus, "What is truth?" (Jn 3:38). Pilate sees only a defenceless prisoner, a casualty of the machinations of the local intrigues, whose truth, speak though he might of another kingdom, is clearly irrelevant to the real world of power and politics. This prisoner simply does not know how the world works. Whose truth is the Roman to believe? The version of the accusers, or that of this accused man? The sorry truth being acted out in the courtyard outside, or the strange truth that is being promised in here?

"What is truth?" ... In refusing to face this other truth, Pilate turns away from him who witnesses to it, and goes outside to contend with the poisonous situation. It is dawning on him that peace could only come by making one more victim:

> He went out to the Jews again and told them, "I find no case against him. But you have a custom that I release someone for you at the Passover. Do you want me to release for you the King of the Jews?" (Jn 18:38–9)

Deaf to the voice of truth, Pilate now tries to make his judgment. He is reduced to hopeless political bargaining. He can find no case against Jesus, so perhaps the traditional Passover amnesty might provide a way out and let them all retire in peace. Here is the possibility of a deft political gesture that would let everyone off the hook. And Pilate becomes an example of the slippery reality of government without any commitment to conscience or hope for anything different. Why not release to them this harmless "King of the Jews"? The accusers of Jesus have ready their reply: " 'Not this man, but Barabbas!' Now Barabbas was a bandit" (Jn 18:40).

For the Jewish leaders, too, any option for the truth was closed. They made their choice for violence — for Barabbas, the bandit, the subverter of Roman rule and their own authority. They were choosing another kingdom. Opt for that kind of violence, choose that kind of deliverance, pursue that kind of truth — and the safety of the temple and the people would be secured.

Turned from the truth, Pilate is reduced to a gesture of political image-making. He must show he is still in charge, even while struggling to placate his antagonists. He has Jesus flogged. He makes his point, even if it is the innocent victim that has to pay the price. And so he lets his soldiers have their way. The bitterness of their lot as part of the force of occupation in this unhappy land now has a target. They would show their contempt for this people that so hated them. They weave a crown of thorns and proceed with a mock coronation, parodying the "Hail Caesar!" of their army drill as they salute this hapless nonentity with "Hail, King of the Jews!" and repeatedly strike him in the face.

Pilate tries again. He has shown who is in charge. While he appreciates their antipathy to the accused, he won't allow these Jews to force his judicial hand. When Jesus is brought out with his mock crown and royal robe, Pilate presents him: "Here is the man!" (Jn 19:5). Could this miserable human being be of any consequence in the power play of the politics of either Jerusalem or Rome? Whatever kings could be there is no royalty here! It is not enough. The temple authorities and police will only be satisfied with a public Roman execution. They shout "Crucify him! Crucify him!" (Jn 19:6).

Later, strange words would be written and another story told about this Jesus, when future believers came to understand the way he had always understood what lay before him: "When you have lifted up the Son of Man, then you will realize that I am he" (Jn 8:28). The humanity of God, "the man", would only be recognised when love had done its utmost.

As Pilate taunts the accusers to illegal action: "Take him yourselves and crucify him; I find no case against him" (Jn 19:6b), a further odd unsettling factor surfaces in their charges: according to their law "he ought to die because he has claimed to be the Son of God" (Jn 19:7).

Here is another dimension; not just a matter of political intrigue about Jewish royalty, but some implication of the presence of the divine. Pilate is out of his depth: "Now when Pilate heard this, he was more afraid than ever" (Jn 19:8). Hearing this change in the charge against the prisoner, the Roman Governor fears that he is being drawn into a horrible calamity. He goes back inside and addresses a different kind of question to this King of the Jews, to this pretended "Son of God": "Where are you from?" (Jn 19:9). His question echoes in the silence of this disturbing man: "Jesus gave him no answer." In the unsettling presence of truth, Pilate resorts to empty threat, "Do you not know that I have power to release you, and power to crucify you?" (Jn 19:10). Neither power seems relevant to this case — especially now when Jesus breaks his silence to say that all power is given "from above" (Jn 19:11), by one who is not restricted to the alternatives Pilate poses. While the Roman official is complicit in the lie and the injustice of what is taking place, he is not the initiator of it: "therefore the one who handed me over to you is guilty of a greater sin" (Jn 19:11). After this strange exoneration, Pilate is confirmed in his efforts to release him ...

Other gospel accounts offer further details. In Luke's, Pilate, when hearing that Jesus is from Galilee, sends him off to Herod whose authority is exercised in that region. But this ploy only delays the moment of truth. Despite further interrogation and mockery in the presence of Herod, Jesus, having said nothing, is returned to Pilate. At least the Roman has the scant consolation of knowing that his duplicitous ally has recognised his action as a conciliatory gesture.

But the charge is reiterated. How can you release a royal pretender in an empire in which it is wise for everyone to acknowledge just who is in charge: "You are no friend of the emperor" (Jn 19:12b). Checkmate for Pilate: he might risk something for this man, but not himself. And so he brings Jesus outside, to the judge's bench on a paved area. John's gospel permits an interpretation that Pilate sits Jesus in the place of honour: "Here is your king!" (Jn 19:14).

It is noon now. When the paschal lambs are being slaughtered in the temple, the guardians of that temple are calling for the blood of this victim, and declaring their allegiance to the emperor. This act of ultimate political chicanery is not only the betrayal of the Jewish law by which they have pretended to judge him. Within a few decades it will result in the destruction of the temple itself when the emperor's armies come to wreak their havoc on the Holy City and its holy place.

And so the paradoxical trial comes to its end, to leave forever the question: Who was being judged?

Defeated by it all, warned by his wife to have nothing to do with this innocent man, washing his hands of the whole thing as the violence threatens to get out of hand, Pilate hands Jesus over. The beleaguered Roman official insisted that his understanding of the charge stand against the objections of the Jewish leaders. The inscription he ordered to be fixed to the cross read, in all the languages of his world — Hebrew, Latin and Greek — "Jesus of Nazareth, the King of the Jews" (Jn 19:19). To the chagrin of those who had plotted his murder, such an inscription spoke of no pretender, not even of a crime, but of a fact. They saw it as a final calculated insult — as though the Roman were implying that this man about to be crucified was of royal status, possessing a nobility beyond anything found in those who wanted to do away with him. True, politics were politics, and Jesus had to go. But Pilate wanted to keep the record straight: "What I have written I have written" (Jn 19:22). Some inkling of a truth he dared not deny had touched him in the end.

Every age is well advised to recognise itself in the dynamics of violence, fear, envy and injustice which carried away this innocent victim those centuries ago. Yet, as we look back over two millennia, we are not dealing with archetypal figures populating a religious mythology. There was a real Jesus of Nazareth. He did not walk above the earth, but on it; he left footprints in the dust of Palestine, and a memory in the minds of friends and adversaries alike. His trial provoked a real commotion in a real city. He posed a real problem for those who administered a real temple. Pilate is a real historical figure — an unimportant official presiding over a minor province of the great empire. The cross was recognised as a gruesome deterrent for subversives and slaves. Its nails pierced real flesh and sinew and nerve. There was a precise moment when the one who hung there died. And his corpse was buried in a real tomb. In all this, too, the real God was at work. Jesus lived and died in a past age. But it remains a familiar world of fear, betrayal, self-interest, political expediency. The truth he witnessed to met head-on the shady world of distorted justice, religious intrigues, political oppression and foreign occupation. He was mocked as a false king by representatives of what has always been thought of as the real world. It had no tolerance for the subversive presence of the God from whom he came. To admit otherwise would mean the end of everything, and a change so complete that nothing could be the same again. The old lies, the usual compromises, made this world run smoothly enough. Life, after this execution, could go on in peace.

In witnessing to the truth, Jesus was not tranquilly enclosed in a religion separate from life. His message came up against a world of politics, and had a political price to pay. Anyone pretending to follow him must accept the consequences. To leave idols behind, to find one's deepest identity in love for others and in responsibility for the poor, eventually makes a political difference. It means a new suffering and a new making: suffering — because the old world does not tolerate such seismic disturbances; and a new making — since faith can never be itself unless it is busy about forming a new social order; even a new politics; certainly a new humanity in God — in that other kingdom in which the innocent and vulnerable are not sacrificed to self-serving power.

VI

On the way to Calvary

The Via Dolorosa has long been celebrated in Christian piety and devotion. Even if a number of the traditional stations are closer to legend than to the events actually recorded in the gospels, they suggest aspects of our experience of the mystery of Christ's love. Not to refer to them would be to deprive Christian imagination today of the contemplative insights of generations of the saints and sinners who have read the gospels before us.

For example, the three falls of Christ on his way to Calvary, which figure in the traditional enumeration of the Stations of the Cross, convey a fundamental Gospel truth. It is this: Jesus' surrender to the Father for the sake of the world's salvation is the result of a choice — on the Father's part in giving us his beloved Son, and on Jesus' part in bearing the whole weight of our human darkness. Jesus' deliberate act is forged in the harshness of human experience. Among the many places in the New Testament where this is referred to is the occasion when Paul calls the Philippians away from any "selfish ambition or conceit", and into an attitude of self-forgetfulness in the service of others, modelled on the example of Jesus. He cites an early Christian hymn saying that Christ Jesus

> *who, though he was in the form of God,*
> *did not regard equality with God*
> *as something to be exploited,*
> *but emptied himself,*
> *taking the form of a slave,*
> *being born in human likeness.*
> *And being found in human form,*
> *he humbled himself*
> *and became obedient to the point of death — even death on*
> *a cross.* (Phil 2:6–8)

The way of Jesus was no glorious path of conquest; for it was marked at every step with a deliberate and loving self-abasement. He gave himself into the darkness and weakness of our human condition. The God he reveals in such lowliness is not a divine being somehow floating above our human world, but one who has compassionately come to meet us, to be with us and alongside us, in the pilgrimage of faith. In its imaginative way, the legend of the three falls of Jesus evokes three facets of the divine compassion. First, Jesus, as the divine Son, steps out of himself in compassion ("[he] emptied himself, taking the form of a slave"). Second, this divine one is "born in human likeness" and "found in human form" in the mystery of the incarnation. He walks with us along our pilgrim way. Third, and this takes us to the heart of the

Passion, he gives himself up to death, even to the ultimate horror of the cross, in his vulnerability to the evils of our world: "he humbled himself ... to the point of death — even death on a cross". When Christian imagination, then, depicts Jesus falling three times beneath the cross even while he presses on to the final moment, it is sensing the compassionate love that has freely and deliberately given itself "for us and our salvation".

If the three falls suggest three aspects of the divine compassion, they also evoke aspects of Jesus' confrontation with the power of evil that reached its culmination on the cross. His determination to serve the cause of his Father, to give himself for our salvation, was at once a consent to the will of God, and a refusal of all that was less than that.

The gospels speak elsewhere of his freedom in terms of his being tested by the devil — the embodiment of our false selves, of the idols we so easily serve, and of a whole culture that would accommodate Jesus for its purposes, provided he left it undisturbed. We see a clear example of this in the wilderness, where the tempter first appealed to Jesus' status as the Son of God to encourage him to turn stone into bread. But his way was not to be the Lord of a consumer society limited to the possession and enjoyment of material goods. Jesus acted in the name of the God of another way and another life: "It is written: 'One does not live by bread alone' " (Lk 4:4). In this respect, the whole Passion story depicts him as falling under the weight of the false expectations of the world.

We are taken deeper into the heart of his freedom when, in the wilderness, Jesus is tempted again, faced with the possibility of possessing purely political power — "all the kingdoms of the world" (Lk 4:5). The devil offers him "their glory and all this authority" (Lk 4:6). If he would only worship the spirit of this world, "it would be yours" (Lk 4:7). Again, in the name of the Father who is offering another kind of kingdom, Jesus refuses: "Worship the Lord your God, and serve only him" (Lk 4:8). In the story of the Passion, too, we see his struggle against the machinations of political ambition and worldly fame.

In the third wilderness temptation the devil entices him to use his divine status to escape from the harsh reality of the world, and so to leave it untouched and undisturbed by the Kingdom of God: "If you are the Son of God, throw yourself down from here" (Lk 4:9) — the angels of God would be summoned to save him from the law of gravity! Against this, Jesus opts to be human with us in the real world in which God acts. He will not reduce God to the status of an agent of self-glorification: "It is written, 'Do not put the Lord your God to the test' " (Lk 4:12). In his carrying of the cross, Jesus falls beneath the weight of a world which, while endlessly creative in making idols for its own glory, remains indifferent to divine glory and resistant to God's will.

The freedom of Jesus in dedicating himself to the cause of his Father means an obedient self-surrender to the divine will, on its terms. To be for God is to be against all that is less than God. The Letter to the Hebrews makes its point:

> Although he was a Son, he learned obedience through what he suffered; and having been made perfect, he became the source of eternal salvation for all who obey him ... (Heb 5:8–9)

When the contemplative imagination of the faith depicts Jesus falling three times beneath the cross, it is in fact describing the reality of the love of God compassionately giving itself into the reality of our world. Jesus is "a forerunner on our behalf" (Heb 6:20) to open "the new and living way" (Heb 10:20). His entire earthly career had followed the direction the Spirit of love inspired. In this last journey of his life he speaks to us still: "I am the way, and the truth, and the life" (Jn 14:6).

In the light of the whole Gospel, as Christian devotion imaginatively ponders Jesus' last agonised steps and the collapse threatening him after hours of torture and mockery, the gospels focus on a number of precious details. It was the Roman custom to make the condemned criminal undergo a final act of public humiliation. The condemned had to carry the cross-beam through the city on the way to the place of execution. This detour was designed to achieve the maximum effect in instructing the populace on the reality of justice. We are told that two criminals were with Jesus on this journey to execution. He was to be in the company of sinners till the end.

As the grim procession of the guards, executioners, official witnesses and the condemned victims wound its way through the Holy City to Golgotha, as Jesus staggered along in their midst, a foreigner, Simon of Cyrene, is press-ganged into a brutal service. He is made to carry the cross. This man, who had migrated to Jerusalem from Northern Africa, is identifiable, at least in one early Christian community, as "the father of Alexander and Rufus" (Mk 15:21). Simon's forced participation in the horrible event that was being enacted would bear fruit. The full significance of the mystery at work in the pain and disgrace of this journey to crucifixion would be recognised by his sons. But at this time, all that was visible to the Cyrenean was the blood-covered criminal being taken to his execution.

It would seem that Simon had been coming in from his farm in the countryside to rest for the sabbath and to prepare for the Passover feast. Then came this brutal interruption. Any hope of rest and festivity was gone for him now, as the local authorities picked him out as the foreigner for a grisly public service. Whatever slender reputation he may have had would be forever tainted by this debasing involvement. His moment of history was one of public humiliation. He would be forever associated with a condemned criminal and the gruesome reality of the cross he was forced to carry. He was not to know that he would be remembered, this father of the early Christians Alexander and Rufus, in another way ...

Was it all a mere accident — the growing weakness of Jesus, and the arrival of Simon on the scene? Why did he attract the guards' attention? Was he the victim of racial prejudice — an African in Jerusalem — or simply regarded as someone so insignificant that no one could possibly object to his being treated in this manner? Had he shouted some word of sympathy, been too curious, or was he simply randomly picked out of the crowd pressing about? These questions can never be answered, even if they remain always worth being asked, at least in later times when the non-persons of our societies have no rights and no honour amongst us. Any society set against the truth of God ends by making victims of its own people. The evil perpetrated by any faction in any society will work to make everyone complicit in its crimes.

Admittedly, all we really know is that he, Simon of Cyrene, was there — in the wrong place and at the wrong time — and that he was considered capable of carrying the cross of the condemned man. The gospels are silent on any further details. Little wonder, however, that believers over the generations have thought of Simon as unwittingly doing what we are all called to do: "Whoever does not carry the cross and follow me cannot be my disciple" (Lk 14:27).

The cross seems always to occur for us in a jagged, random way. No time is ever the right time for any of us to be pulled out of ourselves by the demand to follow Christ. His cross is offered us in the face of the suffering other who meets our eyes, and permits no escape from the question, "What will you do now when you are the only one here to help me?". Our plans and calculations are interrupted with the dreadful otherness of God's will and the demands of our suffering neighbour.

If the cross came to us only as something we could plan, only as a demand we could accommodate, only as enabling us to maintain our present undisturbed self-sufficiency, it would not be the cross at all; nor would it be love for others on the terms on which they need us; nor surrender to the Lord whose kingdom is not of this world. It is a burden and a demand taking us beyond where we would plan to go. It finds us all when, like Simon, we too have finished our work and are looking forward to some rest and festivity, to confront us with the demands of a love that will not let us rest or rejoice until we act. And even then it means finding rest in another kind of peace and another kind of joy. It leaves us feeling foolish and ill-prepared ... but in good company. St Paul writes to his enthusiastic Corinthians:

For I decided to know nothing among you except Jesus Christ, and him crucified ... But we speak God's wisdom, secret and hidden, which God declared before the ages for our glory. None of the rulers of this age understood this; for if they had, they would not have crucified the Lord of glory ... (1 Cor 2:2, 7–8)

The Gospel of Luke records that "a great number of people" (Lk 23:27) followed after Jesus on his way to execution. Perhaps they recognised in him something of themselves — their best selves, exposed and condemned in a harsh dark world of human pride and violence. This anonymous crowd can be taken as a symbol of all innocent nameless victims of history who had followed and will follow him along this path — whether or not he has been or is known to them.

Amongst these were found the women "who were beating their breasts and wailing for him". These especially were pierced by the tragedy that was taking place. They wondered at the kind of world in which they had given birth to their children, where the best and most beautiful values of our humanity were at the mercy of other murderous realities — a world in which neither humanity nor God seemed to count when it really mattered. They lamented the impending execution of this man who had offered them another hope. He had loved their children, seeing in them the tender promise of another kind of life. For him all arguments about who was the greatest was a silly distraction. He had placed one of their children by his side and said, "Whoever welcomes this child in my name welcomes me ... for the least among all of you is the greatest" (Lk 9:47–8). He stood for a world hospitable to the powerless and the innocent, in which their children would be safe. These women could recall the time when they had brought their children to him to receive his blessing, how his disciples, locked into the serious business of their own ambitions, had tried to discourage them. But he had called their children to him and insisted that they be allowed to come, for to such as these who had not learned the ways of violence and ambition "the kingdom of God belongs" (Lk 18:16). To his mind, "whoever does not receive the kingdom of God as a little child will never enter it" (Lk 18:17).

Now that hope was finished, and the age-old violence of the world was about to crush him, Jesus now turns to them, and utters words that seemed in horrible contradiction to what he had promised before:

> Daughters of Jerusalem, do not weep for me, but weep for your-selves and for your children. For the days are surely coming when they will say, "Blessed are the barren, and the wombs that never bore, and the breasts that never nursed". (Lk 23:28–9)

Some dreadful testing reversal of even the most precious forces of life was taking place. Their lamentation over him was a lament for their lost selves in a lost world which had failed to recognise its salvation: "For if they do this when the wood is green, what will happen when it is dry?" (Lk 23:31). If Caiaphas had calculated that it was better for one man to be sacrificed to Roman justice for the sake of peace, there would come a time when those same Romans would make a similar calculation. It would be better for this whole nation to be sacrificed for the sake of the empire. The temple would be destroyed and Jerusalem would be razed. If his own people had turned to Jesus in a way of peace and surrender to God, the kingdoms of violence would have been subverted from within.

But now the politics of violence and envy and victimisation was to go on ...

What will happen ... ? The question is left unanswered. There would be greater darkness yet, and the sorry tale of the world's desolation is not yet over. What light would be left to shine in the coming darkness? All the mothers of all the children who have seen their children die, forgotten in the fierce priorities of war, racial violence, political ambition and greed have felt the darkening of the world. Jesus has meant another world to them. To the women following the cross, he was now going to his end. What hope was left? The promise of a kingdom open to the powerless and the innocent "like little children" had been killed by a world forged by self-serving power.

In the light of what did happen, Christian devotion would imagine two further scenes not mentioned in the Gospel, both dealing with Jewish women who felt the full extent of the tragedy that was taking place. The first recalls how a certain Veronica wiped the face of Jesus, and further legend has it that the imprint of his face was left on the cloth.

Again there is a deep evangelical truth hidden here. By allowing ourselves to be called out of our isolation and to meet the eye of a suffering other, by meeting Jesus in the least of his brothers and sisters, his image is impressed on us, and we conform to Christ in his love.

The second scene is Jesus' meeting with his afflicted mother. It is as though devotion cannot wait till the moment when John's gospel will present her as standing by the cross. Here, too, a deep Gospel truth is evoked. As the Father gives what is most intimate to himself for the world's salvation, his Beloved Son, it is the vocation of Mary, the first disciple, to show forth the boundless love of God in her maternal love, that a new humanity might be born out of such travail. She had lived with the prophecy of Simeon that her son would be "a sign that will be opposed so that the inner thoughts of many will be revealed ... " (Lk 2:34–5). Now the opposition was coming to its climax, and the violence that rules our world was brought into the light, and the ways of hope were to be deprived of every support other than the truth of God. In her surrender to what only love could bring about, Mary's heart is torn: "and a sword will pierce your own soul too" (Lk 2:35). Thus she becomes the model of the compassionate love which, by following Christ as the only way, learns how to wait on God, and not to be turned to hatred and despair in the midst of darkness.

VII

Jesus and
"the Good Thief"

"Jesus, remember me when you come into your kingdom" (Lk 23:42). One of the dying criminals speaks to the dying Jesus in words which express one of the most intimate and touching prayers in all the gospels.

The criminal concerned has been known in popular devotion as "the Good Thief". Such a description is not quite accurate. After all, there is no reason to think of him as "good", since he admits that he has been "justly condemned, for we are getting what we deserve for our deeds" (Lk 23:41). Nor, most probably, was he a thief, since the gospels speak of him as a "wrongdoer" or a "bandit". But he does make a remarkable request. He does not address Jesus in the more customary formal terms — such as "Lord" or "Rabbi" or "Son of David" — but simply as "Jesus", in a directness unparalleled elsewhere in the gospels. Jesus, "this man who has done nothing wrong" (Lk 23:41), is there with him to be called on, despite the wretched fate they both share.

His prayer is a marvellously ironic turn in the story of the Passion. Jesus replies, "Truly I tell you, today you will be with me in Paradise" (Lk 23:43). Given the tragic drama being enacted, it is hardly possible to talk about this gospel's sense of humour. But is it not an extraordinary form of black comedy when a criminal turns to a man being crucified with him to ask his fellow sufferer to remember him when he comes into his kingdom? The irony is all the more piercing when this Jesus assures his companion in torture and execution that on this very day they will be reunited in Paradise. Did the ways of the world that had brought both of them to this desperate point matter so little? How could such a promise be made in the midst of such an unpromising situation?

Up to this point, Luke's gospel has been recounting what amounts to a crescendo of rejection directed against the man who makes this promise — Jesus. But this prayer of the crucified criminal has been preceded by another prayer, that of the crucified Son: "Father, forgive them, for they do not know what they are doing" (Lk 23:34). The prayer of the innocent one to the all-merciful Father who gives to those who ask, who brings home those who search, who opens the door to those who knock, who gives the Holy Spirit to those pray, is now answered. Grace is at work in the prayer of the crucified wrongdoer, in the very fact that he prays, and in the promise that Jesus gives. In the exchange between these two crucified men, the great mystery of all-merciful love is being disclosed.

Divine forgiveness begins to upset and change the world. As the darkness gathers, and the light of the sun itself is dimmed, as the veil of the temple is torn in two, Jesus cries with a loud voice, "Father, into your hands I commend my spirit" (Lk 23:46), and breathes his last. Jesus has gone, to await his fellow sufferer in the paradise of the Father.

Through this final act of surrender the current of divine mercy begins to flow. Lives change. The Roman centurion standing by the cross begins to praise God, declaring in the light of all that has happened, "Certainly this man was innocent" (Lk 23:47). The crowds who had come to witness a gruesome spectacle of justice go away beating their breasts. The tide begins to turn. In the distance, many who knew him, including the women who had followed him from Galilee, stand watching on the fringe of something impossibly new and wonderful.

Joseph of Arimathea, a member of the Jewish Council who had dissented from its actions and is still waiting in hope for the kingdom of God to come, seeks Pilate's authorisation to bury the body of Jesus. His hopes are not exhausted, despite such an obvious end. The watching women now follow him to the tomb, and go off to prepare the spices and ointments for burial. Through the sabbath, they rest, with whatever hopes are left to them.

Then the astonishment and confusion in the early dawn of the next day ... the report of the women to the eleven; Peter's amazement after seeing the empty tomb; the burning hearts of the disciples on the way to Emmaus and their recognition of Christ in the breaking of the bread — and then the appearances of the Risen Lord to the apostles and the community about them so "that repentance and forgiveness of sins ... be proclaimed in his name to all the nations ..." (Lk 24:47).

In the exchange between dying Jesus and the dying criminal, the mercy that would enable hearts to change and sins to be forgiven has already begun its work. The great refusal has been reversed. The time of healing love has come.

VIII

At the foot
of the cross

Golgotha ... "There they crucified him; and with him two others, one on either side, with Jesus between them" (Jn 19:18). As Moses had lifted up the serpent in the desert for the healing of Israel, "so must the Son of Man be lifted up, that whoever believes in him may have eternal life" (Jn 3:14). Here the story reaches the culmination of divine revelation: "When you have lifted up the Son of Man, then you will realise that I am he ... " (Jn 8:28). A judgment had been promised when the rule of death would be reversed, and Jesus would be a magnet drawing all to himself in a new humanity: "Now is the judgment of this world; now the ruler of this world will be driven out. And I, when I am lifted up from the earth, will draw all people to myself" (Jn 12:31-2). Jesus had indicated "the kind of death he was to die" (Jn 12:33), and now it is happening. He is nailed there, dying between two criminals. To all intents and purposes, he is not doing anything — powerless, utterly reduced, not attracting anyone, simply condemned and executed like his two companions.

But John's gospel draws the believer deeper into the God-revealing moment. As we read in chapter 5 Pilate insisted, against the objections of Jesus' accusers, that the cross bear the inscription, in all the languages of the country, "Jesus of Nazareth, the King of the Jews" (Jn 19:19). Precisely at this point Jesus is the manifestation of a love which is given from beyond this world but acts within it to enfold all in its light and power: he is drawing all people to himself. The Father of Jesus is acting "to gather into one the dispersed children of God" (Jn 11:52). Pilate, feeling however obscurely the attractive power of Jesus, at once resists it, and yet becomes its instrument: "What I have written I have written" (Jn 19:22).

The evangelist introduces the strange detail of Jesus' seamless tunic, which the soldiers, having cut up the rest of his clothes, do not wish to divide. This has often since been thought of as symbolic of the unity between Christ and his disciples. It is in this spirit of unity that Jesus prayed at an earlier time:

I ask not only on behalf of these, but also on behalf of those who will believe in me through their word, that they may all be one. As you, Father, are in me, and I am in you, may they also be in us, so that the world may believe that you have sent me. (Jn 17:20–1)

The growing import of this prayer is now unfolded. His mother, and two other women, the other Marys, are standing by his cross. Jesus sees his mother and the Beloved Disciple, the ideal believer, beside her. His previous prayer for the unity of all translates into a loving command: "Woman, here is your son" (Jn 19:26).

His mother had been the first to commit herself to him beyond all human expectations. Now she is summoned to a maternal love for all true believers, in a new family, "to gather into one the dispersed children of God" (Jn 11:52). In drawing all to himself, Jesus gives us to one another in a new unity of love.

In this new world of loving unity, he now addresses the disciple who had reclined next to him at the Last Supper: "Here is your mother" (Jn 19:27). In the emerging infant community of the Church, a mother's love for Jesus is called to be a mother's love for all who belong to him; and a disciple's intimacy with his master is called to be a welcoming love for his fellow believers. Though Jesus will depart to draw us, through his Spirit, to the surrender and adoration of true faith, this woman of faith and this man of faith find support in a mutual love in the community of the Church. True believers are never alone.

John's gospel goes on to tell us that "from that hour the disciple took her into his own home" (Jn 19:27). It is the hour when the Son of Man is glorified, when the grain of wheat falls into the earth to die, not to remain alone but, in dying, to bear much fruit (Jn 12:24).

It is also the hour of passover, when Jesus is to depart from this world and go to the Father, when "having loved his own who were in the world, he loved them to the end" (Jn 13:1).

The gospel story hurries to its pivotal moment. Jesus comes to the fulfilment of his mission, knowing that his end has come: "I am thirsty" (Jn 19:28). He is impatient to drain to the dregs "the cup the Father ha[d] given [him]" (Jn 18:11). Now that the scriptures have been fulfilled, and the moment for his return to the Father has come, he dies with the triumphant cry: "It is finished" (Jn 19:30). He had now built the holy space of a new temple — where heaven would be opened, when in this final hour true believers "will worship the Father in spirit and in truth (Jn 4:23). To the truth of God, he had given witness in life and in death; and now, he hands over the Spirit. Then "he bow[s] his head and [gives] up the Spirit" (Jn 19:30).

On Mary, on the Beloved Disciple, on the other women gathered at the foot of the cross, the Spirit is poured out. Not only do they have one another in the unity of faith and love. For now they are given "the Spirit of truth whom the world cannot receive" (Jn 14:17), "the Advocate, the Holy Spirit whom the Father will send in my name, will teach you everything and remind you of all that I have said to you" (Jn 14:26), "who will testify on my behalf" (Jn 15:26), "who will prove the world wrong about sin and righteousness and judgment ... " (Jn 16:8).

The Church will always have to face its own wavering. Love will grow cold and faith will grow weak. But the Spirit of truth will continue to give witness. Sin, the perversion of the human heart at work in rejecting Jesus, will be brought to light. Human righteousness, in those who "loved human glory more than the glory that comes from God" (Jn 12:43), is now confounded. The Father glorifies the crucified Jesus as his Son. And the crucified one is lifted up in judgment. He is the sign of another kingdom raised against "the ruler of this world". This world, hitherto governed by its idols and enclosed in death, will now be forever disturbed by the breath of true life.

But Jesus hangs now as a corpse on the cross. One of the soldiers, officially certifying his death, drives a spear into his side, from which "blood and water" flow. So insistent is the testimony of the evangelist at this point — "His testimony is true, and he knows that he tells the truth" (Jn 19:35) — that believers are invited to see the water and blood flowing from the pierced side of Jesus as special signs of the current of the new life that Jesus gives. The water flowing from Christ's wounded side indicates the life-giving and cleansing waters of baptism: "No one can enter the kingdom of God without being born of water and Spirit" (Jn 3:5). The blood that runs down is a symbol of the blood of Christ offered in the eucharistic cup: "Those who eat my flesh and drink my blood abide in me, and I in them" (Jn 6:56).

Though Jesus has returned to the Father, he continues to purify and nourish the Church in the sacraments of enduring presence. To the mind of John, the blood and water flowing down Christ's side toward the representatives of the Church gathered there are a marvellous indicator of the beginning of a new age; an assurance that Jesus will be present to the Church through all the time of faith. The "rivers of living water" (Jn 7:38) now flow; the Spirit has been given; and Jesus draws all to himself as the light of the world.

You who have been redeemed, consider who it is who hangs on the cross for you, whose death gives life to the dead, whose passing is mourned by heaven and earth, while even the hard stones are split. Consider how great he is; consider what he is.

In order that the Church might be formed from the side of Christ as he slept on the cross, in order that the word of Scripture might be fulfilled, "They shall look on him whom they have pierced", God's providence decreed that one of the soldiers should open his sacred side with a spear so that the blood and water might flow out to pay the price of our salvation. This blood, which flowed from its source in the secret recesses of his heart, gave the sacraments of the Church power to confer the life of grace, and for those who already live in Christ was already a draught of living water welling up to eternal life.[1]

[1] St Bonaventure, *Opusc.* 3, 29–30.47, as found in the Office of Readings for the Feast of the Sacred Heart, *The Divine Office III*, Sydney, E.J. Dwyer, 1974, 50–1.

IX

Jesus dies on the cross

In the cross, two kingdoms clash. The ruler of this world, the lie that infects all cultures and societies, confronts the truth of another king and another kingdom. Who and what is being judged? In crucifying this man — this Jesus, who, in the name of the one true God, had offered our humanity a life without end in union with God — the self-destructiveness of sin and evil is revealed. The powers of darkness go into a final spasm, seeking to rid our common conscience of what so fundamentally disturbs it. In the midst of this darkness, a love not of this world continues on its own terms. It works only in the power of what it is, revealed as a love that keeps on being love no matter what the rejection it suffers.

The cross was an obscene reality in the ancient world. It was a mode of execution reserved for slaves and subverters of the empire, designed to deter any threat to the imperial peace. Only when crucifixion as a form of execution had been abolished by

Constantine three hundred years later would the cross become a Christian symbol. Any of us today who would gladly wear a cross as an emblem of Christian commitment can hardly imagine the degree of emotional revulsion resulting from connecting divine revelation with such a hideous form of death. That the divine being could reveal itself in such a way had to be experienced as religious scandal and a philosophical folly — "a stumbling block to the Jews and foolishness to Gentiles" (1 Cor 1:23). The cross of Christ was the most radical form of culture shock. Surely God could not be, could not act, like that! Surely God could not come to us as a criminal executed by imperial Rome.

Yet precisely at this point of utter dismay and revulsion, the sheer excess of divine mercy and compassion was displayed. In the cross of Jesus the excess of our human capacity for evil was outwitted by that excess of love on God's part which not "anything else in all creation" (Rom 8:39) could counter. In the providence of love working in and through all events of our history, the most demonic gesture of human evil is used to dramatise the ecstatic extravagance of God's mercy on sinful humanity: "Christ died for the ungodly ... God proves his love for us in that while we still were sinners Christ died for us" (Rom 5:6, 8).

The love of Christ goes to an unimaginable limit, to reach us at that point where our history is found to be most against God, most enclosed in the vicious circle of violence and despair. For those who would be united in a new humanity living in the death-less life of this other kingdom, no matter who they were or how-ever great their sins, here was the divine breakthrough into the world at the furthermost limit of its alienation from God: "to those who are the called, both Jews and Greeks, Christ the power of God and the wisdom of God" (1 Cor 1:24).

The impossible possibilities of divine love are manifested in this most innocent of the world's victims. Let the powers of this world do as they will, let evil display its most demonic intensity, this truth will stand: when he is lifted up, he will draw all to himself (Jn 12:32). For here was "God's wisdom, secret and hidden, which God decreed before the ages for our glory" (1 Cor 2:7). So surprisingly hidden is the wisdom of love concealed in this crucified man that "none of the rulers of this age understood this; for if they had they would not have crucified the Lord of glory" (1 Cor 2:8). Evil hides from itself its own destructiveness. Unable to imagine any reality beyond itself, it is closed in its own defeat. But there is another, a divine imagination at work: "Father, forgive them, for they do not know what they are doing" (Lk 23:34).

In the decades that followed the crucifixion, the first generation of Christians had their own experience of weakness and persecution. They lovingly contemplated the cross as the disclosure of the wisdom of God. By unmasking our capacities to destroy and deface our true selves, it brought about a great reversal. It stood for a new beginning. God would not add evil to evil by wreaking divine vengeance on sinful humanity. For, through the cross, a greater good would use this evil for its own loving purpose; and a way would be opened to turn the sin-enclosed world to God.

Jesus knew our evils. The Word had truly become flesh and dwelt amongst us. As a mortal man he suffered death, to be swallowed up into the silence, darkness, poverty, powerlessness and separation that mark all our dying. In his death there were the further intensities of suffering: agony of mind and body, betrayal, abandonment, condemnation, torture, mockery, failure, execution ...

He suffered death as one put to death, with everything wrapped in the greatest darkness of all, the sense of the terrifying absence of God in an impenetrably God-forsaken world.

The cross is the climax of the power of darkness. God appears to have been banished from his good creation, just as that creation appears shut in its own malice and hopelessness. In condemning the Son to the cross, the injustice of the world appears as just; and the crucified Son, far from being accepted as the bringer of the kingdom and the true form of our humanity, appears as a criminal. He has become "a curse for us — for it is written 'Cursed is everyone who hangs on a tree' " (Gal 3:13). When John's gospel invites its readers, in Pilate's words, to "behold the man" (Jn 19:6), it implies a judgment on our standard versions of humanity. The inflated projections of human pride are exploded by the cross of the Word incarnate.

The reality of his cross is the focus of all the enigmatic experiences that make up the "problem of evil": the defencelessness of the good, the absence of God, the immorality of "morality", the human perversity of preferring to cause death rather than allow for life ... The cross stands as the sign of a world disowning its own grace and promise. It wrings from the crucified an agonised prayer, "Eloi, Eloi, lema sabachthani? [My God, My God, why hast thou abandoned me?]", and culminates in his loud last cry as he breathes his last (Mk 15:34-7). Mark does not let us forget that any hope we have is built on Jesus' experience of the starkness of a death in that real world where infinite love appears as the most defenceless, the most hopelessly unreal of truths.

Other gospel accounts present the cross as the high point of the freedom of Jesus, as he makes his ultimate surrender: "Father, into your hands I commend my spirit" (Lk 23:46), and "It is finished" (Jn 19:30). He yields himself to an incalculable mystery of grace so that God's grace may the more abound — even at this most impenetrable point of the world's darkness. To meditate on the Passion of Christ is to be drawn into the drama of his naked self-surrender.

The cross discloses for believers the ultimate, the final reality of God. In killing Jesus it is as though the power of evil challenges the mystery of God to reveal itself. It defies God to be truly God. God would not be God if love were defeated here. And God would have been defeated if the Father of mercies were to be finally reduced to the level of worldly power play, by answering evil with evil, and so making "an eye for an eye and a tooth for a tooth" a cosmic law binding even the Father himself.

As this Son prays for the forgiveness of those who have crucified him, he rejects any worldly identity, any worldly justification or protection save what the Father can be for him. At the point of demonic concentration of evil, he surrenders himself to an all-Holy Spirit as the last breath of his life. This Spirit, inspiring the self-giving death of Christ for the many, has no other identity, works in no other power, than that of unconditional love. The trinitarian communion of self-sacrificing love brings a new crucified humanity into existence.

By dying on the cross, the man of parables becomes the supreme parable, of how God undoes the evil of the world, and forms our humanity anew.

X

The grace of the cross

How each of us hears the story of the Passion, how each of us, with the gaze of the heart, looks at that bruised face, how each of us finds the cross unveiled in the secret places of our lives: such issues are not a matter of lofty theological theory. We must look elsewhere. We turn to the witness of all those who have been drawn, in different ways, to the whole truth and found it to be the healing truth, revealed in him who has been lifted up before the world "to gather into one the scattered children of God" (Jn 11:53).

The liturgy of Good Friday invites us to let down our defences before God. We must allow ourselves simply to behold Jesus, and even each other, with a heart disarmed. The liturgy of this day suggests that the way of the Church is always a grave procession to the cross, where the whole truth, the healing truth, is displayed before us. When the heart of faith follows Jesus in his Passion to the end, it begins to feel again. In a movement of gracious sympathy we are put in touch with the depths of suffering that so often hide the inarticulate — in each of our lives, in the Church itself, in the world at large.

"Behold the wood of the cross on which hung the Saviour of the world." As the cross is unveiled and we come to venerate it — to kiss it or touch it or bow before it — hearts are touched, warmed by a threefold grace.

First, we begin to sense the overwhelming passion of God: "For God so loved the world that he gave his only Son ... " (Jn 3:16). The cross points upward. From the foot of the cross, we lift our eyes, and see the terrible form of the crucified silhouetted against a horizon formed by all our questions, all our fears and all our hopes. The cross focuses our gaze on the heart of God. By contemplating the wounded body hanging before us, we are in the presence of the incomprehensible love that has reached out into the world to find us. In the darkness another light has begun to shine. We find ourselves standing in the radiance of that Father who gave what is most intimate and revealing of himself, "the only Son", into the pain and darkness and deadly violence of the world of our making. We find ourselves, not looking up into an empty, dreadful space marked only by a cross, but meeting the gaze of an inexhaustible love that has come and found us, and given itself.

Paul, the great apostle of such grace, went so far as to call the cross God's folly and weakness (1 Cor 1:25). Such is the foolishness and vulnerability of what our unawakened hearts know is too good to be true. Yet, in being foolish as God is foolish, to adore such love, to yield to it, to live and move and work with it, is to find in all our days an ever richer, deeper, more complete answer to the question: "Who will separate us from the love of Christ?" (Rom 8:35). Not God, surely. Nor anything in all God's creation — nothing we suffer or enjoy; nothing buried in our past, nor looming in the future; nothing in our most private fears, nor anything moving in the great powers that shape our world ... No, not anything we are, or were, or will be; not anything we have done or left unfinished or undone — nothing in the whole of creation is able to separate us from the love God has shown us in Christ Jesus (Rom 8:39).

In the cross, in the Passion of Christ, the heart of God is revealed. An infinite love has gone to the limits. The Holy Spirit is the ecstasy of love and mercy in which God is turned to the world. In the depths of our tragedies is a passion in which the Holy Trinity has felt our sufferings its own. Showing a remarkable instinct for this truth, Christian tradition has taught us to make the sign of the cross "in the name of the Father, and of the Son, and of the Holy Spirit".

In such grace, faith adores, surrenders and gives thanks. In the words of the Good Friday liturgy: "This is the wood of the cross on which hung the Saviour of the world. Come, let us worship."

There is a second grace, but it is not immediately obvious. As the cross points up to God, its arms point out to the world. We see embodied in the crucified Jesus the whole agony and pain of our world. Enfleshed in him are all the sufferings of the innocent, even the more dreadful sufferings of the guilty, as he bore our sins. Hammered into him is the fate of the powerless, of the condemned, of the lost and the broken and the hopeless — the useless ones of the world — all who dwell in the shadow of death, all who go through the bitter valley of the world's dark night.

This does not reflect a distant, philosophising or consoling religion. All our theories are driven to distraction once we meet the eye of even one of the uncounted millions who have gone down in defeat. There are the dear ones whom we have loved, whose lives seemed to have been loaded with impossible suffering and incredible tragedy ... and beyond them, the anonymous crowds of the slave camps, of the mass graves, of starving children — the poor, the tortured, the detritus of history, the victims buried under the rubble of bombed cities; the young for whom this world has no place; the old who have lost what place they had ... "We adore you, O Christ," says the Liturgy of Good Friday, "and we praise you, because by your holy cross, you have redeemed the world".

Yet here too the cross is grace for us. It jolts us out of ourselves to be joined, as a brother or sister, to the immense family of all who suffer, in tenderness, compassion and generous deeds. Such compassion is a gift, given beyond any worldly calculation. The cross of Jesus points to fellowship of suffering and demands that we bear one another's burdens. It points to a path which, for good reason, we fear to travel — toward those places and people where life offers no success, where martyrs give their lives, where hearts are broken, and the darkness lies thick on all the world. Yet go we must:

Come you that are blessed by my Father, inherit the kingdom prepared for you from the foundation of the world; for I was hungry and you gave me food, I was thirsty and you gave me something to drink, I was a stranger and you welcomed me, I was naked and you gave me clothing, I was sick and you took care of me, I was in prison and you visited me. (Mt 25:34–6)

The cross of Jesus involves us in the suffering of all, forever troubling our lives with the demands of compassion: "Just as you did it to one of the least of these who are members of my family, you did it to me" (Mt 25:40).

The cross pointing up and out, also points down — a third grace reflecting that, like the second, may at first elude us. In that direction, too, lies a dreaded place — the depths of our own selves. To look on the cross, to consider the unimaginable shame and utter defeat of such an execution, it could be that we see ourselves revealed in failure in all its forms: the defeat of the years, the love that somehow passed us by, the holiness that became more and more a distant ideal, the essential secret of life that we feel we never heard, the promises we made but could never keep — all ending in a kind of condemned cell of isolation which neither God nor anyone else can penetrate. We are hunched there, unable to love and to pray, unsure of where we went wrong, unable to utter our guilt or our need or our hopes ...

How could we dare speak of grace here? Unless there is one who has gone before us, who is present even here in this haunted place to hear our prayer, we are left with nothing but our lost selves. Yet the grace of the Gospel whispers its hope even where no other voice can reach ... If we, left with nothing but what God can be for us as our loveless pretensions collapse about us, now move toward him, in a humility carved into us by the pressure of life's temptations and failures, and go down into the very pit of what we think of as loneliness, we will find him waiting: "Come to me, all you that are weary and are carrying heavy burdens, and I will give you rest" (Mt 11:28).

Rest, there; refreshment; a new beginning; a renewed passion for everything all along we knew we were called to: "Truly I tell you, today you will be with me in Paradise" (Lk 23:43).

XI

Holy Saturday

Over seventeen centuries ago, an unknown preacher posed a question to his hearers about the meaning of this day:

> What is happening? Today there is a great silence over the earth, a great silence and stillness, a great silence because the King sleeps; the earth was in terror and was still, because God slept in the flesh and raised up those who were sleeping from the ages. God has died in the flesh, and the underworld has trembled.[1]

The great hopeful conviction of Christian hope was forged in the face of a terrible ending. The body of the dead Jesus lay hanging on the cross.

---

[1] The second reading from the Office of Readings for Holy Saturday, *The Divine Office II*, Sydney, E.J. Dwyer, 1974, 320–1 (PG 43, 440A–452C).

If the corpse of a crucified criminal were left exposed it would have desecrated that sabbath's Preparation festival (Jn 19:31) and polluted the land. In this case, it is the crucified Jesus who is hanging there; in his life, condemned as a subverter of the temple worship; in his death, a potential defiler of the holy day. Both enemy and friend wanted him buried. In the event, Pilate gave permission to Joseph of Arimathea to take away his body:

> So Joseph took the body and wrapped it in a clean linen cloth and laid it in his own new tomb, which he had hewn in the rock. He then rolled a great stone to the door of the tomb and went away. (Mt 27:59–60)

The great stone had been rolled into place while devout women watched, but the Jewish authorities prevailed upon Pilate to send a guard to the place of burial: "So they went with the guard and made the tomb secure by sealing the stone" (Mt 27:66). Jesus is dead, buried, laid to rest in a rocky grave which his disciple, Joseph, had excavated for himself.

In a cosmic sense, Jesus lies buried in all our graves. Can any hope survive? Can any new hope spring forth? Though Christians will, indeed, come to live in the joy of an answer to these questions, what was then clear is that hope had to take its time. It must wait through the whole length of this longest day when Jesus is truly dead among the dead — dead and buried, cut off from the land of the living, an executed criminal, gone from this world in failure and shame, knowing no divine vindication.

The liturgy of this day prescribes that our alleluias be silent, that the altars of our churches lie stripped and the tabernacle stand empty. If our sorrow is to be turned to joy, hope must learn how to wait, to express the grief out of which it is born. On this day, we are stripped, along with Jesus, of everything save what God can be and what God can do in God's good time.

This day of waiting extends through the whole of human history. A great stone lies heavy on the graves of the uncountable dead. Human history has witnessed the killing of many martyrs. So many hopes have been buried. The tombs of peacemakers have always been carefully guarded. Their spirits must not escape to accuse the violent of their crimes. What had they been hoping for?

In all the imagination of great art, in all the inspiration of poetry and music, in all the fervour of religious faith, what have we been waiting for? Have we simply been fabricating images of ourselves to compensate for a void of meaninglessness? Are our hopes merely projections of ourselves thrown onto a blank screen for fear that there is no answer, no meaning, no final truth? Is faith merely setting up one more idol in history's crazy hall of mirrors? Or may we really see in the crucified Jesus an icon, the face of the living God, back-lit by a light not of this world, holding us in a loving gaze?

Hidden in the silence and grief of this sabbath when the hopes of all the world are at stake is the conviction that Jesus, the beloved Son, is one with us not only on the surface of life, not only in the experience of life's mortal agonies, but also in going down into the underworld of the dead. With the burial of that tortured body, the God of Jesus too is apparently buried. Where have our hopes gone?

With Jesus dead and buried, the image of his Father is blotted out, and the power of his Spirit reduced to impotence. Where is

God now? Jesus lies in the grave. He had proclaimed the reign of God, a realm of grace in which God would lift up the poor and the outcast. But that kingdom has not come. With Jesus dead and buried, one more hopeless failure has been added to the sum of hopeless failures, those who failed to adapt to the way things are and ever will be. The poor have possessed no kingdom; the mourning have received no comfort; the meek have not inherited the earth; those hungering for justice are still famished; the merciful have found no answering mercy; the pure of heart see no God in this place of burial; the peacemakers remain God's orphaned children; and those persecuted in the cause of goodness have made no difference ...

Jesus is buried in a black hole. Faith and hope and love, all the deepest God-ward direction of our lives, are swallowed up and brought to nothing.

In contemplating the brutalised corpse of Jesus, our hearts cannot but recall the dreadful finality of the deaths of all those we have loved and cared for. For this Saturday, this middle day, was not originally experienced as the middle of anything. It was the day of God's obvious defeat and banishment from the world. The Word was reduced to silence. All those who had once thrilled in wonder at the promise he gave were now numbed and bewildered in a universe turned bleak and grotesque.

There is a puzzling phrase in the Apostle's Creed, "He descended into hell". In the language of faith, the believer professes faith in Jesus Christ as the "only Son" of the Father and as "Our Lord", who, "conceived by the power of the Holy Spirit and born of the

Virgin Mary", enters the world not only as a human being with us, but as one who "suffered under Pontius Pilate, was crucified, died, and was buried". A cross and a tomb in the Palestine of a particular time under a particular Roman administration mark the fact that he lived, died, and was buried at that time, in that place. But the creed goes on. Jesus has been with us not only on the surface of life, not only in the agony of suffering and disgrace, not only in the grave, but to a mysterious further extent: "He descended into hell"[2].

What is this hell which Jesus goes down into? "Hell" translates the Greek Hades, the god whose name is "Unseen", ruling over the underworld. The word hell is often used to translate the Hebrew Sheol, meaning literally "the place of questioning". The realm of the dead has always left the human mind wondering, appalled at the fate of those who have gone from this life. The Old Testament describes it as the abode of "darkness", "silence", "dust", "the place of no return"; a total separation from life and, indeed, even from God. It was an underworld of inaction and lifelessness (Eccl 9:10), of sadness (Sir 14:11–17), of powerlessness (Isa 14:10), and even of no praise of God (Ps 6:5; Ps 88:3–6, 16). Linked with the Canaanite imagery of Mot, the god of death, it was the place where the dead were swallowed up and devoured (Isa 5:14). Death's appetite is never satisfied (Prov 30:16). All life's radiance and power come to nothing (Isa 14:10–19).

More soberly, the Latin of the Apostle's Creed inferna, or infera, seems to mean simply "the lowest places" that human imagination can depict, the depths of God-forsakenness in which we have no obvious human hope. Jesus has gone down into the regions of

---

[2] See the *Catechism of the Catholic Church*, Liguori Publications, Liguori: 49 and 164–5.

ultimate dread, the point most distant from God. He has entered a darkness that leaves the imagination appalled, where all theories are useless, where death reigns unchallenged in all its lethal power to silence, to separate and destroy.

Jesus, in surrender to the Father's will, descends to the point furthermost from God; where death reigns. He dies as one accursed, condemned by the law of Israel, rejected by his own people, executed as a criminal by the imperial power, seemingly abandoned by the God whose reign he proclaimed — his prayers unanswered, his disciples scattered.

Haunting the silence of this day when Jesus lies buried is this question: Can the ultimate love he proclaimed reach him, and those who follow him, at this impenetrable depth? Does his tomb sealed with the great stone set the final limit on all life and love, even on the power of God?

But God works. The Word must become flesh — right to the end, and be reduced to utter silence. The communion between the Father and the Son is stretched to breaking point. The love that is God shows itself to be infinite compassion for the lost. The Father sends his beloved Son into this realm of apparent God-forsakenness. Nothing can span that distance except the spirit of a love that knows no bounds. Only if such love can survive at the most deadly point of death can it promise a new creation.

In his descent into darkness, Jesus becomes God's way of reaching out to the dead, to the hopeless, to the irretrievably lost. In his descent to this depth he brings all the compassion of God. The Father has given what is most intimate to himself, the beloved Son, to the point furthermost from him. Love has gone to the end.

Truly, he goes to seek out our first parent like a lost sheep; he wishes to visit those who sit in darkness and in the shadow of death. He goes to free the prisoner Adam, from his pains, and his fellow-prisoner, Eve, — he who is God and Adam's Son ... "Awake, O sleeper and arise from the dead, and Christ shall give you light!"[3]

The sense of this point of ultimate enigma and dread is conveyed in the many references (over fifty) that the New Testament makes to Jesus being raised "from the dead", *ek nekron*. The mystery of Holy Saturday lies in Jesus' total obedience to the Father's will. He goes down into these most dreaded, deepest reaches of human darkness. He is with the dead in all their powerlessness.

On this day, hope begins to rally at the point where all seems lost. It begins to rise up through the way that love has opened. While philosophy and theology will always puzzle over the manner in which the freedom of God respects our human freedom, in Jesus' death and burial among the dead Christian hope finds an image of the inexpressible creativity of divine love. Human freedom, even in a state of ultimate perversion, even when it is frozen in resistance against the power and claims of the infinite Other, now finds that this Other is with it in unreserved forgiveness. Love continues to offer itself even when it is most rejected. Christ is *inferno profundior*, "deeper than the lowest place" (Gregory the Great).

However we human beings, with our burdens of guilt and dread, imagine this lowest place to which Jesus descends on this longest day, faith can now share the conviction of St Paul:

For if we have been united with him in a death like his, we will certainly be united with him in a resurrection like his. We know

---

[3] From the homily already quoted, *The Divine Office II*, 321.

that our old self was crucified with him so that the body of sin might be destroyed, and we might no longer be enslaved to sin. But if we have died with Christ, we believe that we will also live with him. We know that Christ, being raised from the dead, will never die again; death no longer has dominion over him. The death he died, he died to sin, once for all; but the life he lives, he lives to God. So you also must consider yourselves dead to sin and alive to God in Christ Jesus. (Rom 6:5–11)

The place of ultimate estrangement is now open to another presence — the only presence that could penetrate it — that of an absolute love giving itself, as the Father so loves the world as to give his only Son. The compassion of God fills all the dimensions of human existence: "in Christ God was reconciling the world to himself, not counting their trespasses against them ..." (2 Cor 5:19). The dimensions of the cross span the whole abyss into which we can fall. The Lord of life has been there; even there. Jesus has changed the realm of death into a place of meeting. No part of our experience, no corner of the universe, is closed to an all-merciful love. Love moves through the whole of creation to offer hope where no hope is to be found.

I am your God who for your sake became your son, who for you and your descendants now speak, and command with authority those in prison: Come forth; and those in darkness, Have light; and those who sleep, Rise.

I command you, "Awake, sleeper. I have not made you to be held a prisoner in the underworld. Arise from the dead. I am the life of the dead. Arise, O man, work of my hands, arise, you who were fashioned in my image, Rise, let us go hence." For you in me, and I in you, together we are one undivided person.[4]

To the eyes of hope, Jesus is buried that he might ascend, to fill the heights and depths of the created world: he "fills all things", descending even to the "lower parts of the earth" (Eph 4:6). He is Lord of the dead, and holds in his hands the keys of death and Sheol (Rev 1:18). Every knee bows to him, even those "under the earth" (Phil 2:10). The Son of Man, three days and three nights in the heart of the earth, is Jesus, the new Jonah (Mt 12:40). Though he is swallowed up by the monster of death, though he descends into the abyss (Rom 10:6–8), against him the gates of Sheol shall not prevail (Mt 16:18; 27:51–3). He has the power to put into subjection death as the last enemy (1 Cor 15:26–9). After his death, he preaches to the mysterious "spirits in prison" (1 Pet 3:18–20), and to all the dead (1 Pet 4:6). Freed "from death" (Acts 2:24), he is "the firstborn of all creation" (Col 1:15) — "the firstborn from the dead" (Col 1:18).

Through him, the loving compassion of God is extended throughout the whole universe. As this boundless love stirs in our hearts to unsettle our familiar versions of hope and despair, it leads us to declare that the Friday of crucifixion was indeed "Good"; and that this Saturday, this longest day of waiting, is indeed "Holy":

The cherubim throne has been prepared, the bearers are ready and waiting, the bridal chamber is in order, the food is provided, the everlasting houses and rooms are in readiness, the treasures of good things have been opened; the kingdom of heaven has been prepared before the ages.[5]

---

4 From the same homily, The Divine Office II, 522.
5 Conclusion of the homily quoted above, The Divine Office II, 522.

XII

The empty tomb

Early on the first day of the week, while it was still dark, Mary Magdalene came to the tomb and saw that the stone had been removed ... (Jn 20:1)

The first day of the new week of God's creation ... But it is still dark. Faith has to pass through its long day and dark night. Magdalene has come to the tomb. She finds to her horror and confusion that the stone has been taken away. She runs immediately to Peter and to the Beloved Disciple.

The meeting of these three is a precious moment in the Church's journey to full-bodied faith. Magdalene reports that "they" — all the violent forces that had condemned and crucified her master — have now succeeded in even taking away his body. She speaks for all the disciples, who were left at a loss in the events of that time: "We do not know where they have laid him" (Jn 20:2).

The grieving disciples have now lost all contact with Jesus who had been so horribly separated from them. The reported emptiness of his tomb serves only to increase the emptiness within them. Their last hold on the former reality has been broken.

While Peter and the Beloved Disciple set out immediately for the tomb as if to verify their loss, we, at this later stage of the Church, can accompany them on what will be a path of faith. They both run, but the Beloved Disciple arrives at the burial site first. Through the ages, Christian contemplation has found in his speed the vigour that came from his special intimacy with Christ. The disciple bends down and looks in. He sees only the linen burial cloths; and waits for Peter to arrive. The way of faith is the way of the whole Church, even if it moves more slowly and requires patience on the part of all. Still, it leads to a clearer vision of what is there to be believed. The disciple then enters after Peter, and notes not only the linen wrappings, but the head-cloth, another part of the material that had shrouded the mortal remains of Jesus, rolled up in a separate place. In that empty darkness, the light of faith begins to shine: "He saw and believed" (Jn 20:8). Not only has the stone been taken away, but the wrappings of death are also unravelled. Such was not so in the case of Lazarus when Jesus called him forth from the tomb (Jn 11:44). Lazarus was restored to this life, after which he would finally die, still bound by the power of death. But Jesus is not bound; he is risen, to be the source of deathless life — though the full story of God's love, giving life in such a death, had yet to be fully understood in the light of the scriptures and the Spirit's witness.

After Peter and the other disciple have "returned to their homes" (Jn 20:10), Mary Magdalene is left alone in her desolation. Darkness and emptiness are still all that is obvious to her.

Through her tears, she too looks in. But this time she sees not merely grave-cloths in the darkness of the tomb. There is radiance there — two messengers of God, "angels in white", the awesome fringe of a glory that is to be revealed. She is asked, "Woman, why are you weeping?" (Jn 20:13). She is not to know how later generations will recall the promise made by him whose mortal remains she is seeking, about how heaven would be made open and the believer would see "the angels of God ascending and descending upon the Son of Man" (Jn 1:51). She is not yet at that moment of vision. The stone still lies heavy on her heart, enclosing her in sadness.

The loving irony of the evangelist invites us now to note a further step in Magdalene's journey of faith. She must be a witness for all who will come to believe. She turns around, looking away from the tomb, and sees Jesus standing there. She does not recognise him; her eyes are still not habituated to the new light that has begun to shine. She is faced with another question, this time from him: "Woman, why are you weeping? Whom are you looking for?" (Jn 20:15).

God is present in our lives at the edge of our real questions. Jesus is always a question for us. At the beginning of John's gospel, the first words spoken by Jesus are: "What are you looking for?" (Jn 1:38). What is Magdalene really looking for now?

The irony deepens. For Mary now supposes Jesus to be the gardener, a party to the violent forces that had removed him from her. She pleads with the still-unrecognised Jesus to tell her where the body has been concealed so that she can take him away and give him a decent burial. But the Good Shepherd, who knows his

sheep by name (Jn 10:3), now addresses her by name: "Miriam!";
and all the intimacy of former times breaks out in her answer:
"'Rabbouni!' (which means Teacher)" (Jn 20:16). She tries to embrace
him, to hold on to the way things were. But now the freedom of
faith demands more. She must not cling to the Jesus she had
known, no matter how tender her previous attachment had been:
"Do not hold on to me, because I have not yet ascended to the
Father" (Jn 20:17). The climactic hour of Jesus' glorification is still in
progress in which he will be revealed as the light of the world. In
this hour, Magdalene is not to cling to the past, but is called to
become a maker of the future — "Go to my brothers" — with the
message from Jesus, "I am ascending to my Father and your Father,
to my God and your God" (Jn 20:17). The disciples are now no longer
servants but friends, no longer even disciples, but brothers and sisters of Jesus in the one communion of new life. Life now moves in
a heaven opened to all who will believe and enter it.

In the darkness and emptiness of the tomb, Mary has been
changed. She is no longer a casualty in a terrible defeat but a witness to true life. Once reproached by the radiant angels in the
tomb for her blind grief, she becomes herself a heaven-sent messenger of joy: "Mary Magdalene went and announced to the disciples, 'I have seen the Lord'; and she told them that he had said
these things to her" (Jn 20:18).

It never was, nor could it ever be, that Christian faith could find
its energy in the mere fact of an empty tomb. There was no point in
seeking the living among the dead. The joy of the disciples arose
from their encounter with the crucified Lord, now living and life-

giving. Once they have believed, they show no inclination to haunt a grave-site. Faith now consists in a full-bodied connection with the risen Jesus who had been buried as a crucified criminal. The accounts of the empty tomb in the Gospel prevent our faith from being a nice construction placed on a terrible reality. But the empty tomb does stand as a kind of historical marker for the reality of "the life" now revealed and offered to all. It expresses a demand — set right there in the history of human defeat and failure — for faith to wake to its full potential. The empty tomb points away from itself. The absence of the body of Jesus promises a new presence; the emptiness of his tomb witnesses to a new fullness of contact; a grave-site opens beyond itself to a whole universe transformed.

Faith comes to the tomb, not to stay there, but to break forth into a new sense of wonder. Because he is risen, everything is changed; the universe is now different. To enter into this empty tomb is to be challenged to stake all on the real victory of God's life-giving love. In the light of that truth, the sting of death has been drawn (Acts 2:31; 1 Cor 15:54).

The empty tomb plants the seeds of questioning in the solid ground of history. It is profoundly disturbing for any version of a world hermetically sealed against the extravagances of love. It points to another reality; and if there is an argument against it, it is because it is too good to be true. If it were true, everything would have to change.

The emptiness of the tomb underscores the advantage of Jesus' going away (Jn 16:7). Not defeated by death, no longer buried behind the great stone, no longer bound in the shrouds of death, no longer restricted to the expectations or fears or grief of disciples, Jesus lives, a source of life for all. The grain of wheat, falling into the ground and dying, has not remained alone (Jn 12:24).

XIII

He is risen!

When it was evening on that day, the first day of the week, and the doors of the house where the disciples had met were locked for fear of the Jews, Jesus came and stood among them and said, "Peace be with you." After he said this, he showed them his hands and his side. Then the disciples rejoiced when they saw the Lord. Jesus said to them again, "Peace be with you. As the Father has sent me, so I send you." When he had said this, he breathed on them and said to them, "Receive the Holy Spirit. If you forgive the sins of any, they are forgiven them; if you retain the sins of any, they are retained." (Jn 20:19–23)

It was now toward the end of that day of astonishing good news. The stone had been taken away, the tomb was empty, the wrappings of death had been unwound, Magdalene had come with her wonderful message. And yet that day was ending, and darkness was returning. Despite the joy of the disciples, the powers that had crucified him were still abroad. He had ascended to the Father, but they were still where they always were. He had gone into glory, but they were locked in their old fears. He had escaped from death, but had they? He was changed, but how changed was their world? Into the locked room of this fear Jesus now comes. He stands among them and gives them the greeting of peace. On one level, it is the *shalom* of normal Jewish greeting; but now it means something more. His previous words spring into new life:

> My peace I give to you. I do not give to you as the world gives. Do not let your hearts be troubled, and do not let them be afraid. You heard me say to you, "I am going away, and I am coming to you". (Jn 14:27–8)

Standing in their midst, he is the embodiment of the peace not of this world. Their hearts, once crushed and broken with fear and grief, now open to a new gift, the peace of the Risen One among them. His departure from them in death is now revealed as a new coming to them in a peace that no human violence can negate. Yet, for his disciples there would still be the fear of persecution in a world antagonistic toward him and them; they and the future generations of believers would continue to be faced with their own frailty. But in his peace there was fundamental assurance. The peace of his presence would continue, no matter how troubled the times would be. He had come "that you may have peace. In the world you will face persecution. But take courage; I have conquered the world" (Jn 16:33).

He who had conquered the world now comes to these who are still very much in the world. Yet he comes from beyond death —

from where death is no longer the all-limiting power. He comes in the power of the reign of God. He comes as the bearer of forgiveness. Neither the evils we suffer nor the evils we cause are the last word any more.

He shows them the wounds in his hands and his side (Jn 20:20). The marks of the cross have become radiant signs of life crying out to God for resurrection. His wounds show the powerlessness of the evil that had been unleashed to do away with him. The scars of the nails and the spear are now emblems of a life so endless and abundant, so founded in God, that the wounds of death can be displayed as a badge of victory. In the wounds of the crucified Jesus, now risen and present to them, the disciples see that our human existence, despite all its struggle and pain and violence, is capable of redemption. For the human story of violence is now subverted from within. The cross of Jesus is the Trojan horse in which the irresistible powers of God's peace, forgiveness and love lie concealed.

> It was fitting that God ... in bringing many children to glory, should make the pioneer of their salvation perfect through sufferings ... For this reason Jesus is not ashamed to call them brothers and sisters ... Since, therefore, the children share flesh and blood, he himself likewise shared the same things, so that through death he might destroy the one who has the power of death, that is, the devil, and free those who all their lives were held in slavery by the fear of death. (Heb 2:10–15)

"Then the disciples rejoiced when they saw the Lord" (Jn 20:20b). Their sorrow had been turned into joy. The crucified one now lived, and the joy of the life he embodied overflowed from him, and brimmed over within them: "I have said these things to you that my joy may be in you, and that your joy may be complete" (Jn 15:11).

Jesus speaks again: another greeting of peace from the Risen Lord (Jn 20:21). From now on, peace received must be given to others, in a life of peace-making. As the disciples enjoy the peace of Jesus' presence and thrill with the joy of his life, they must enter now into the outgoing movement of his mission: "As the Father has sent me, so I send you" (Jn 20:21). As branches of the living vine (Jn 15:5), they are to bear fruit in the world in witnessing to the truth of the love that has been revealed. The peace of Christ is a peace open to all in a life of communion with God ...

But the atmosphere of the locked room still holds a sober memory of the fear and defeat in which the disciples have been enclosed. So now Jesus breathes another Spirit into them. This Holy Spirit had been given, as his last breath, to Mary and John at the foot of the cross. Now it is given to the expanding Church of the generations to come: "Receive the Holy Spirit" (Jn 20:22) — the breath of a new holiness, of a new peace and unity for humankind in God. In the power of this gift, "if you forgive the sins of any, they are forgiven them ... " (Jn 20:23). Having received the gift of merciful love, the disciples are to be its agents in the world.

But Christ goes on: "If you retain the sins of any, they are retained" (Jn 20:23). At first, this would seem almost a mean restriction on the joy of this new beginning. Yet these words of the Lord remind his followers that the peace he gives is not a false peace. It is not a pretence. It does not cover over deceit, hatred and human pride. Love will not settle for anything less than freedom in those to whom it is offered. It will not be used as a convenient consolation for those who would come to God on their own terms. Love will allow anyone to deny the truth.

The Breath of holiness which Jesus communicates to his disciples demands that they confront the world, contesting the violence that rules it, name its crimes and stand with its victims. Sent by Jesus, his followers are now agents of the Spirit who was sent to "prove the world wrong about sin and righteousness and judgment" (Jn 16:8). If the world is to receive the gift of God's love, our self-justifying ways must yield to another judgment. For the world to deny Jesus — whom it crucified as a criminal but who is now risen from the dead — would mean for it to be hopelessly locked in the domain of death. Christians, in the world yet not of it, in the peace they offer and the truth they tell in Christ's name, are the bearers of another life. This life promises no peace and no joy, but only disturbance and judgment, to those who hide in darkness from the light that now shines. The Risen One upsets the self-enclosed world; and neither its judgments nor its tombs can hold him.

The resurrection of Jesus does not distract faith into an otherworldly domain. Believers must engage their world in its reality — which will include persecution for them and a continuing resistance to the truth of Christ himself. Yet despite the inevitable conflict and risk that threaten, "the darkness is passing away and the true light is already shining" (1 Jn 2:8). From the Risen One, an expanding circle of community unfolds to include all peoples, and even the whole of creation. The disciples are sent into the world with the consciousness of being part of the new humanity already realised in Christ. To share in the humanity of the Risen Jesus means to receive and to offer the love and forgiveness we have received. Violent relationships based on envy and vengeance are abolished as Christ explodes the vicious circle of all our hatreds. Even the emblematic antagonism existing between Israel as "God's Chosen People" and the rest of the nations of the world is healed at its root. Peace has broken out. St Paul, in his letter to the Ephesians, in reference to the healing peace that Christ is for all, proclaims:

> For he is our peace; in his flesh he has made both groups into one, and has broken down the dividing wall, that is the hostility between us ... So he came and proclaimed peace to those who were far off and peace to those who were near, for through him both of us have access in one Spirit to the Father. (Eph 2:14–18)

Into that locked room of all our fears Jesus has come. The Spirit has been breathed forth. For the disciples there is peace and rejoicing as the energies of new life begin to stir; and they are sent by the Risen One into the world with the power of new life. They have seen the Lord.

But Thomas had not been there with them when Jesus came (Jn 20:24). As he enters into this room luminous now with the wonder of what has taken place, he holds back — and states his own conditions for believing: "Unless I see the mark of the nails in his hands, and put my finger in the mark of the nails and my hand in his side, I will not believe" (Jn 20:25). For him the stone still encloses the corpse of the Crucified, and the binding cloths of death still wrap him round. The dark reality of the tomb still chills the heart of this disciple. Like Mary Magdalene before him, Thomas still clings to the Jesus he has known.

Believers from earliest times have found in this disciple, called "the Twin" (Jn 20:24), something akin to their own hesitations and fears. Thomas is related to us all when we find ourselves insisting that the Risen Lord must fit into our limited worlds, and not we into his ...

One week later, once more on the "Day of the Lord" as the

114

earliest generations of Christians would call their Sundays, the disciples are gathered behind closed doors, and the recalcitrant Thomas is with them. And so is Jesus. He comes and stands among them, again with his greeting of peace. He confronts Thomas; and in loving sympathy for the hesitations and ambiguities which all generations of believers know, Jesus then offers to meet the conditions his apostle had imposed: "Put your finger here and see my hands. Reach out your hand and put it in my side" (Jn 20:27). Yet the Risen One utters the summons to go further: "Do not doubt but believe" (Jn 20:27).

Now all Thomas' conditions fall away. In an ecstatic act of faith, he leaves behind all the criteria he had imposed on how God could act. The stone is removed from his heart; the wrappings of death are unwound; the tomb is empty. This moment in this room, like every moment in every place where believers gather, is filled with the presence of the Crucified and Risen One. In the ecstasy of faith, Thomas goes beyond the world of his own calculations to enter the universe of deathless love and unbounded grace: "My Lord and my God!" (Jn 20:28). Here, now, he finds the Word who was "in the beginning", the Word who was "with God" and "was God" (Jn 1:1). The disciple sees how the Son of Man has been lifted up to be revealed as "I am he" (Jn 8:28), as the unique revelation of the Father. All his past experience of the master he had followed and of the God he had sought to serve comes together as he recalls the words of Jesus: "The Father is in me and I am in the Father" (Jn 10:38). In Jesus he finds his Lord and his God.

Though Thomas had borne the burden of our human hesitations, the ever-present Risen Lord invites us all into the full freedom and joy of true faith: "Blessed are those who have not seen and yet have come to believe" (Jn 20:29).

The Crucified is risen. He is present to the Church in the water and the blood of baptism and the eucharist. He has breathed the Holy Spirit into his disciples to send them into the world as he was sent, into a world that we now experience as larger and perhaps more threatening than the world of ages past. But when we believers today illumine our experience by meditating on the word of Scripture, we enter into a holy communion made up of many witnesses; like the Beloved Disciple, we receive Mary, the first of the disciples, into our home. Likewise, Peter experienced the misery of his own weakness and came to confess to the Lord, that we might find new courage. Magdalene, too, found her way from grief to joy, the disciples overcame their fear, and the resistance of Thomas fell away, that we might continue to believe, familiar with both their darkness and their light.

In that great communion around the Risen Jesus, the words of one of these first believers find their way into our hearts, these twenty centuries later:

> We declare to you what was from the beginning, what we have heard, what we have seen with our eyes, what we have looked at and touched with our hands, concerning the word of life — this life was revealed, and we have seen and testify to it, and declare to you the eternal life that was with the Father and was revealed to us — we declare to you what we have seen and heard so that you also may have fellowship with us; and truly our fellowship is with the Father and with his Son Jesus Christ. We are writing these things so that our joy may be complete. (1 Jn 1:1–4)

XIV

The universe transformed

Rejoice, heavenly powers, sing, choirs of angels! Exult, all creation around God's throne! Jesus Christ, our King, is risen!
  Rejoice, O earth, in shining splendour, radiant in the brightness of your King! Christ has conquered! Glory fills you! Darkness vanishes forever![1]

As the *Exultet* sings every Easter Vigil, the whole of creation rejoices. The power of the resurrection already touches everything in the universe. In and with the risen Jesus the earth rejoices, clothed in the brightness of eternal communion with God. In the depths of all creation, the heart of the Risen One is the centre of a new vitality. It is the heart of love; the pulse of new, ultimate life beats there. In him the whole of creation awakes to find itself to be heaven-in-the-making.

---

[1] From the *Exultet*, the Liturgy of the Easter Vigil.

While the actual body of the Risen Lord is no longer visible and palpable, Christ has not ceased to be incarnate in the world of God's creation. The whole of creation is contained in the risen humanity of Christ, even though the full glory of this event is yet to be revealed. Paul prays that the Christian community of Colossae will show the patience and joy appropriate to the great transformation that has occurred:

> May you be made strong with all the strength that comes from his glorious power, and may you be prepared to endure everything with patience, while joyfully giving thanks to the Father, who has enabled you to share in the inheritance of the saints in the light. He has rescued us from the power of darkness and transferred us into the kingdom of his beloved Son, in whom we have redemption, the forgiveness of sins. (Col 1:11–14)

This illumination of mind and heart and the sense of wonderful release flowing from the resurrection are graces affecting not only our human relationship to God, but also our relationship to everything — the whole of creation. In the Risen Lord, the whole universe has been called home:

> He is the image of the invisible God, the firstborn of all creation; for in him all things in heaven and on earth were created ... He himself is before all things, and in him all things hold together.
> (Col 1:15–17)

Christ Jesus remains still embodied in the cosmos, as "the firstborn of all creation", even though he is no longer subjected to the conditions of earthly life. To a new and final extent Christ is present in the totality of the world. When the scriptures speak of him as "Lord", "Head", "the New Adam", "the firstborn of all creation", "the first born from the dead", these early documents of faith present him as "before" all things, the one in whom all reality coheres and finds its fulfilment: "in him all things hold together" (Col 1:17). Not only has the merciful love of God broken through to our world, but our world, irrevocably united to him, breaks through to its ultimate destiny. In him "the ends of the ages" have come upon us (1 Cor 10:11). St Ambrose captures this cosmic sense of the resurrection in his statement, "In Christ, the world has risen, heaven has risen, the earth has risen".[2]

Today, in the knowledge science has given us, we stand in wonder at the great process that has brought us forth over an unimaginable expanse of time. NASA's 1992 COBE satellite has given human eyes the sight to peer back fifteen billion years to our cosmic beginnings. We can have some sense of the blazing fireball of our origins, as it unfurls into billions of galaxies, and condenses into the elements which at this moment are firing the energies of our brains and the beating of our hearts, in all our happy capacities to wonder and to hope.

We are the first generation to have such a vision of the origin of our universe. In accepting such a past, we understand ourselves, despite our different histories and life-stories, to be united in the fifteen-billion-year-old story of the emergence of the universe. Our "common clay" is now recognised as stardust, a cosmic fallout uniting human, animal, plant and mineral as the outcome of a great event. Phosphorus formed in the heart of the stars gives us the skeletons that structure our bodies. The stellar iron enters

---

[2] Ambrose of Milan, *De Excessu Fratris Sui* I, 2 PL 16, 1344.

our blood. The sodium and potassium that drive signals along our nerves are part of a larger message. The cosmic flame of hydrogen burns in our brains. Carbon molecules fuel our metabolism. Our lungs breathe an inspired past ...

Such is the prelude to any appreciation of the amazing creativity of our own planet Earth. To look back over those four and a half billion years to the origin of our planet is to witness a vast cauldron of activity in which the basic chemicals necessary for life were brewed. As this elemental matter slowly cooled to crystallise and condense, it combined and grew in complexity until some marvellous point was reached at which primitive life emerged in the oceans. Out of these oceans came, in their time, creatures of the shore, of estuaries and marshes, to spread eventually over dry land, to take root in the soil, to float or fly in the air, to move on paw or hoof or foot in their various habitats, each to occupy a special place in the life of our planet. Finally, there comes the human, the most complex arrival in the amazingly productive history of the Earth.

The universe rejoices, then, in all the marvellous leaps and transformations that have taken place within it. Our specifically human history has been a long, creative struggle against the forces of entropy and death. We human beings are always living beyond ourselves in hope for a more complete life.

Yet despite all the achievements of art and science, of thought and culture, death continues to mock human achievement, and our highest aspirations have to deal with the overwhelming forces of human evil and self-destruction. Human freedom is continuously being checked, frustrated, appalled by that over which it has no power. The physical laws of mortality and the historical movements of progress and decline assert themselves as a negativity against which we are powerless. The universe can seem so essentially indifferent to human achievement, so uncaring of the individual destiny or cultural attainments, that our greatest sages can see it all as vanity with "nothing new under the sun" (Eccl 1:9). It is all doomed to an eventual and total collapse. Does diminishment, death, exhaustion conquer all?

In the resurrection of the crucified Jesus human hope finds a final assurance. Another energy is at work — a limitless love that nothing in creation can resist or diminish. God "is God not of the dead, but of the living" (Mk 12:27).

In Christ's rising from the dead a universal transformation has occurred. What we most cherish is no longer at the mercy of what we least value or what we most fear. True life has been revealed as stronger than death. At the heart of all things, there is the energy of an infinite love. St Paul sums up this gracious sense of the universe: "All things are yours ... whether ... the world or life or death or the present or the future — all belong to you, and you belong to Christ, and Christ belongs to God" (1 Cor 3:22).

The resurrection does not cancel Jesus' presence to all creation. He holds everything and everyone in the power of deathless life. He belongs to the whole, containing it in his risen form of life. True life is not subject to the power of death and the destructive forces it symbolises: "Christ being raised from the dead will never die again. Death no longer has dominion over him" (Rom 6:9).

The Way of the Cross becomes in the end a path travelled by the whole universe, a way in which our hearts and minds expand to include everything and everyone in the love we have found revealed. The exultant words of a saintly preacher of fifteen centuries ago leave us today with a question: Is our hope big enough, really worthy of the love that has found us?

Through Christ's resurrection, the underworld is opened; through the neophytes of the Church, the world is renewed; heaven is unlocked through the Holy Spirit. For the underworld is opened and gives back the dead; earth is renewed, and from it springs the crop of those who are risen; heaven is unlocked and receives them as they ascend.

So the good thief ascends to paradise; the bodies of the saints enter the holy city; the dead return to the living; and sharing, as it were, Christ's resurrection, all the elements tend upward ... By a single process the Saviour's passion raises from the depths, lifts up from the earth, and places on high.

For Christ's resurrection is life for the dead, pardon for sinners, glory for the saints ...

And so, my brothers and sisters, we ought to rejoice on this holy day. No one should exclude themselves from the general rejoicing because they have sins on their conscience. No one should refuse to take part in the public worship because of the burden of their misdeeds. However great a sinner they may be, on this day they should not despair of pardon, for the privileges granted on this day are great. If a thief was thought worthy of paradise, why should not a Christian be thought worthy of forgiveness?[3]

---

[3] From the sermons of St Maximus of Turin, Sermon 53, 1–2.4, *The Divine Office II*, the Office of Readings, Fifth Sunday of Eastertide, 580–2.